THE DISPOSITION OF UTOPIA WRIGHT

Rahson Sumter

First Edition, 2008
ISBN 13: 978-0-9794472-0-4
ISBN 10: 0-9794472-0-4
Copyright © 2008 by Rahson Sumter

THE MANCHESTER BOOK GROUP
JAMAICA, NY 11431
USA

Email: rahson.sumter@gmail.com
www.joogroup.com

THE DISPOSITION OF UTOPIA WRIGHT

Rahson Sumter

First Edition: 2008
ISBN 13: 978-0-9794472-0-4
ISBN 10: 0-9794472-0-8
Copyright © 2008 by Rahson Sumter

THE MANCHESTER PEARL GROUP
JAMAICA, NY 11431
USA

Email: rahson.sumter@gmail.com
www.utopiawright.com

Printed in India by Cyberwit.net

For my Grandmother her children and
her children's children.

CONTENTS

"It's sad when someone you know becomes someone you knew."

– Joseph L. Mankiewicz

GLORIA

Spending all available time
With this mature woman most would
Overlook, as for me, she completes my
Way of life, bringing all my
Adolescent ignorance to a close,
At most, she loves me in many ways
I can't comprehend,
Thrilled to see her face
In the morning, before
The glory of my endless
Day begins,
She speaks of my life,
As one would preach
Of the coming of Christ,
Rising under the same sun,
I was unable to recognize,
Cleansing her skin
With the same water
I took for granted,
Pampered as a blessing,
Her love unmatched

GLORIA'S DEFINITION

Nothing popular
about her,
So simply put she's just
enough woman to understand,
Sitting before me,
Doing what she does,
A daydreamer at most, an active listener,
Finding reason in all things living,
A woman's
Woman, A molded version
Of a childhood dream, that
Always made me late for school,
I'm honored to be
The friend behind her
Confessions, the lover on
Which she relies,
Providing the same love
And respect she showers me with,
Missing my wife so much,
Missing her touch,
I love that woman

GLORIFIED

In touch with her words,
Unlike my own,
Hers were truthful,
Gradually forming a
Communication,
Unlikely we fought,
Reading to one another
Allowed us to love
Each other,
Too selfish,
We broke free,
Gloria, a woman
Mothered by hate
And raised by deception,
All to prove what
She describes as a point,
Satisfying, from her
Hips to her smile,
Her vanity and denial,
All but allowed her to
Mask the reality of being
Branded, by this crazy
Thing called love

GLORIOUS

A classic flow
Of in and out, special
For her type, a groove
Slow, yet hard,
The satisfaction, written on
Her face, explains
All the misery of her
Prior lovers, a fear
Of intimacy, passed down
By her father, who raped
Her for years, a woman
Fucked over, by the
Many who feel she's
Too passive, an anger
She feels, every time
She's reminded of those
Men and woman, wanting
Her to do the things
They assume was
Best for her, this
Woman I love most,
My best friend, always my wife,
She is glorious

GLOROMA

I love you with the most
Respect, ever given to
A woman,
I cry for you,
Send prayers to our Lord,
For us both, hoping one day,
You will never have to see
Me in such conditions, I love you,
Mostly during the evening
When man is most
Vulnerable, I remain
Man enough to deliver
On the last promise
Between you and I, a secret
We hold close, till death does us dirty
I'm here for good, just understand
That time has changed me
And life on the inside,
Without you, is the hardest
Compensation I'm forced
To deal with

GLORIA'S PERCEPTION

She stands
There, a vision of Angelica,
Pleasing of all vices,
She is my disposition, She is my downfall,
She is not my mother, nor
My sister, whom I've loved, since
Premature birth,
She is not the woman I always
Figured would leave me,
only she can say things so hateful,
Tears begin as I write,
I Can't continue,
I'm done until
This emotion passes

GLORIA'S GOD

It took me four
Years to understand,
Why I shot a man
In the face
And on that last day,
I fell further to
The floor and prayed
To my God for the
First time,
In short God said,
It was me, whose
Life He meant to take,
And with time,
He feels his decision
Will show me the way,
And if properly cared
For, I can walk the
Earth like Jesus did,
And lead the many
Non-believers to His
Palms, in return,
He'll return me to
The arms of my wife,
Whom He believes to be,
The most glorifying
Creature, He has ever
Had the pleasure
Of creating

HER LAST

Fraudulent are
The eyes when
Actions are revealed,
A relationship built
To last more than
A million years,
Has been tainted,
A communication
Between lovers,
Has soured,
How inconsiderate of
This woman, undoing
A happy home,
Yet beneath the lies,
Holds the irony
That she loves
Her man without
End, what else
To say when
Words spoken,
Fall on deaf ears

FORTUNATE

I rode the late train home early, to
Sit close and listen to the words
Only she could propose, such greatness
Hadn't been justified by human laws,
An abnormal physical attraction,
Such as ours had not yet been
Classified, or else I'd be lost
Amongst men who'd want to take
Her from our happy home, promising
Her sexual pleasure I'd dare not,
Therefore I'm honored and some what
Blessed, to be last on a long list
Of men pleased by Gloria's touch

WALL TO WALL

Such a beautiful time behind you, seductively
Pressed, pleasing from wall to wall, a real man
Understood by a woman's touch, gradually
Loving each other, eyes closed,
 Blushing to the world,
Smiles of companionship,
An ocean view of nostalgic lovemaking, a tall tale
Distance from home and or place of conception, a kiss
Hidden between lips,
A taste way too familiar, it becomes a reality, a faded
Love narrated by our children, they suffer most, they
Deserve more, a thin line broken, crushed for its purity,
Shaken and poured, fed to our children as a fury of false
Hope, a core of violence subjected to one tenant,
Annoying to a disturbance,
There they go again, Utopia and Gloria Wright

PURSUIT OF HAPPINESS

The last battle between Gloria and I ended in blood,
The motive of insecurities pierced her face with
A slap, I still regret till this day, Her soul, now forever stuck on The street's
grime, a grind of sexual favors and drugs, broken Promises and thugs, those
who care nothing about her well being, yet She praises these dudes, so sad
to hear through scribes that she's so
Far gone and my kids are the one's who suffer most,
How unfortunate our lives have turned out,
I truly envy the free

JUST A THOUGHT

A baby face, precious
Yet cautious of her
Stimulation, I wait
In a patience,
Admiration sets
From a far, always
Around her, I'm
Falling for her slow,
Her mood becomes
My gain, I enjoy her
Attitude, this woman,
Most find beautiful
Just on general purpose,
On posture alone,
She's envied, her
Personality is stable,
Nothing to brag about,
Yet her sexuality
Is worth stalking,
I'm just talking,
Merely a time
With myself, lovely
I am, Utopia

MISTRESS

She hates the fact
That I think of you
So much, besides that,
I miss you, I'm thinking
Of you almost all my days,
Wishing times were different
And opportunity was avail,
However, I'm committed to her
And she'll always be there,
And you, I lust for, there's no
Way one can compare, amazing how
Love comes and goes,
Hoping one day you'll understand that,
Timing determines all

FATHER

Her glamour is
My own, her mouth
Speaks words I use
And she swears
By my name,
Loving me whole,
Without a fraction
Of guilt, sharing her
Life with me
Because she loves
My company and
Grace, so if
One day I'm no
Longer here and
Life has vacated
My lungs, she
Can proudly say
To our children,
That she loved
A man put here
To lead his family
From their births
To his death

DURING PREGNANCY

It all started when I
Disrespected her in front of
Her loved ones, gathered safe at
The dinner table, full of grace,
I spoke on issues she frowned upon
And left a new impression
On her family, which she resented me for,
I must have crossed many lines,
Unaware of the direction my
Conversation was headed, I
Continued to speak of
Indiscretions my wife had
Forced me to bring to light,
And with that, I wasn't allowed
To speak at family engagements,
Sparking the first of many
Spats between Gloria and I

CRAZED LOVE

You're really the love of
A life so precious, it burns
To question why it has
Been cut short in
Such a horrible way,
A real prince I was,
A man with his balls
Gripped tight, watching
All sorts of men fake
Their way to your heart,
Yet it was I who you
Made love to daily,
It was I who held
You close to my chest
With a squeeze, secure
Enough that both your
Parents accepted me for
Just for being me,
Those were the days,
You and I whispering
Nothings about nothing,
Yet understanding every
Single word said,
Suddenly a bond
Uncertain formed between
You and another, leaving
Me home to wonder, you then pushed
Buttons I prayed you wouldn't

THE LAST ASSUMPTION OF GLORIA WRIGHT

She's reminded of a family tradition passed down
From her mother, who pleased her father and friends coming Home from the
war, With her body, only a child's eyes can Explain the hurt, the countless
rapes, an Attempt to take Her own life was at hand, lost in the suicidal mist,
her last gift was shipped off to prison and she hasn't been The same since,
Glorious Gloria is now an abandoned Building, away from pleasure inherited
and Traditional, selling her sex for survival, losing her focus on life due To
time, as it Moves forward the harder it is, the stronger I get, the weaker
Gloria becomes, the Opposite of life's Trials begins and ends with man,
woman and child, once tainted, the only relief is death found in the streets of
New York City or the custody of New York State

W

These honorable men fought to end
The reign of a government
And their objectives toward the
People's way of life, finally understanding,
Without hate, there's no love
And without war, there's no reason
To fight for a country divided by indifference,
Institutionalized racism and greed,
Now aware and able to speak from within,
These wise men and women stand
20 million strong, behind the laws of God
Preaching to the people
A new way of life found in the North

BROKEN ENGLISH

Hidden behind justice, peace
And equality, is the disturbing truth
Of hypocrisy, lies and greed,
Unheard are the prayers,
Representing the image of maturity,
Standing united to live in a world
Divided by race, religion and money,
Yet expected to fight and resist the
Temptations of freedom,
Unless willing to sacrifice everything
Worth loving per diem

ONE

While sterilized
Momentarily depression invaded the
Time, all were unhappily reminded
Of their brand new surroundings,
Grounded in debt, the impression left
Was dreadful enough to break
Stride, even children were on their knees with
Hands out, not mature enough
To understand the world in which they live,
A culture of people taken by
Missionary force, unable
To break free, their cries heard
In the whisper of the night,
Throughout the north side
Of the South Bronx, where the Hispanics
Too, inhale the same misery most
Tried to deny for the past 450 years,
But prayer overruled each beating,
Sending hope of progression to the people,
That no longer, can one race
Dominate, be dominated or
Separated for the rest to be equal

NOT YET RELEASED

Unforgotten is the
Mental abuse obtained and
Financed by the state
Of New York, where proper
Care is inspected in short seconds,
Lasting longer on paper than
In actual time, yet we must fight
For what is important, while separating
The molested from the monstrous,
All while planning an escape
From this carnival
Controlling our lives

CRIMINOLOGY

The actions executed
Explained the rage
Sheltered, for many years
I dealt with this inner demon
Trapped inside,
Foreshadowed is the graphic
Violence demonstrated
By the beast inside me,
These devils love my
Representation of
Various acts of crime,
Unaware that my disposition is
Disturbing the sleep of others,
Eventually what transpires,
Ends in someone's death,
Framed in public to be seen by
The general population,   .
As a sigh for help

REVITALIZED

A solider of Jesus placed
Her hand on my shoulder and
Explained to me life, through the
Eyes of Christ, through her words
I realized my mistake wasn't my crime,
It was guidance I was lacking, eventually
She detached me from a world of violence and
Wished me on my way, with faith as a guiding tool
And love as a discipline

MOCKINGBIRD

A story never heard has
Many endings, never told,
Funny how life unfolds into
Desperation, reminding the
Soul of its sole purpose,
Underlined and redefined,
Yet reinvented to be
Indefinitely divine,
This story of mine is
Softly spoken to ensure
The truth is told and not
 Misrepresented,
Misspelled and conveyed
To the many few, who
Edit life, with their own
Perception of truth

MEDIUMS

All victims share stories, attentive
To the lies separating them from reunion,
Between children and wives,
Through and through we live through it,
Searching for identification,
Questioning foolish theories, nothing
Better than hell on earth

THE CORNER

You can lose your life
Messing with them boys on
Them corners, yes them corners,
Where the most beautiful children
Walk through life, enjoying the
Corner for its purpose, a family within
A family, the corner is where its
At, on them corners, some never make
It back, others move on to correction facilities,
Where the corner's finest come together to enjoy
Each other's company, the corner will always be,
It is what it is, some find love on
Them corners where children grow into adults,
The corner where fast money is made,
Churches hand pick some of their most
Loyal clergy from them corners, when it
Comes to murder, the corner is where
The police go first, leave it to the corner
To never change, yet don't leave
It to the corner to raise your kids

DR. KING REDUX

Black men and
Woman, black jeans,
Black face and black eyes,
Blackened to a brick
Brown shade of black,
Black men in their prime,
Blackest of the best
Black man before himself,
Properly chosen to bring
Back the black pride,
Missing from the black
People living in
The Untied Sates Of
America, pure blackness
Put back to the top
Of existence, crowned
For his blackness, black
Is what black does

MMM

The million men
Who walked slowly,
Posed no threat
To themselves
Or the many
Who watched from
Their homes,
And they are the
Million men I love
To respectfully
Acknowledge, if
Not for them I'd
Continue my suffering
Long after my
Death

MOCKINGBIRD SINGS

The black stone,
Hurled by the
Protesters of the
Roman Catholic
Church, never meant
To hurt their intended
Receiver, but if
The past is a reminder
Of the present,
Then there's nothing left
To be said because
Freedom is a motive,
Worth fighting for,
The lack of sleep,
Proves the dedication
To the cause,
Not all men can
Pretend life
Showers them with
Blessing after blessing

KING ME

The boarding area
To heaven is scarce
And the people seem scared
Of their last judgment, there
Seems to be a gossip
Spreading about the response
Time of our savior,
But I know these men
Are not that stupid,
A rumor could never
Penetrate God's given
Gesture of life,
All it took was a sign to the
People that the Lord
Was coming, up and
Running were the liars
Sent forth to spread hate,
Separate the righteous
From their goals,
And God fearing people
From their faith

FULTON AND WASHINGTON

The dark complexion
Of this man instilled
Instant fear, walking
Alone down a street
Foreign to his own
Community, the panic
Ran through him,
As his knees fell
To his feet,
He walked slowly
To the corner
With his head
Lowered to
The street,
Hoping never to make
Eye contact with
The locals drinking
That malt liquor
They crave with no end

PUBLICITY

There's no remedy for pleasure
Sought in a tangled web of foreplay,
When the sexual urge isn't to please
At all, but to fornicate, except if the
Lovemaking is vivid enough to
Videotape and release to the public,
This sensitive side of ones animalistic
Nature is tasteless to view, yet I question
How many of the few live such pleasurable
Lives, when the aftermath of it all, lasts
Only but a Short eight seconds

PERCEPTION OF SOUND

Music lost its passion
Somewhere between us
Scratching and pawing
At the doors of heaven
And missing out on the
Spiritual guidance of voice,
Song and inspiration found
In music notes and words,
Adapted to a tone creating
Enjoyable sounds or melodies of our
Pain and or happiness, which can only be
Found in the emotion of sound

LIVING COLORED

Justified love is
Staring us all
In the face,
Yet we shine
Our faith
On false idols
And misleading
Ideologies,
My apologies to the
Unknown lost in the biblical
Times of Jamison Pratt,
Through prayer
And acceptance his
Words will send
A message worth
More than life,
Just believe and you'll
See the gift, be the gift
And live the life,
Destined for you
And those you love

ME

Society made him what
They labeled him as a man,
A child growing up poor,
Yet enriched with support gained
From a society where one's ability to
Survive has its limits from birth,
From Oakland to Harlem,
The faces of the naked truth
Are unfortunate to experience,
A break or two, if only the
Eyes, heart and mind would open
Up to the journey ahead and continue
To fight for what he fought
For when he was me

"Being Alive will eventually kill you."

– **Utopia Wright**

THE BOULEVARD

Graves are hidden
Behind the post office
On St James Place,
Just right of Sanchez
And Poramo Park,
An urban street
War zone, something
Sour to the worst,
Just barely an inch
Of peace, suffering
Is a normal breeze,
Poking the people
With problem after
Problem, fairly not
Something to boast,
Unfortunately
I'll have someone
Meet you at the
Subway station between
Paramus and Pope

PERCY SMALLS

For the love of him he can't remember
A damn thing, all he knows is that
He woke up in a holding cell
With blood all over his hands,
Murder was the case, God bless
Him only, he's going to need all
The prayers he can get, another
Youth hiding behind
The barrel of a pistol,
Now confined to life in
Prison, just the way the ball
Bounces for some, his name is
Percy Smalls, one
Of the unfortunate living
Life inside the beast

FLOODED GRIEF

She managed by
playing cards, idle hands
Kept her focused on
A life other than the
One she once shared,
She doesn't flinch at all,
Fire burns her flesh,
Yet she brushes it off,
Wanting only her man,
Her statue of great things
Past, she's permanently
Sleepless without him,
At old age she vacates
To the mountains and
Stops, no one to admire,
She retires to a slow,
Lonely pension of a death

PHILOSOPHY

Lately I've been sleeping
With ease, a pleasure
I've never experienced, since
My experience here began,
A turn of events, formerly
Known as rehabilitation,
I must be the first to admit
This structure system
Is all in my head, a belief,
Theory that maybe I'm
Not the criminal I'd thought,
Biting a bullet,
I am Utopia Wright

THESE MEN

These men kill for sport
Easily, these men can care less,
These same individuals wanting
Your ass, these same men
Stalking your daughter
On her way to school,
The men will take her
Virginity blood and all,
The same men who you
Fear, seem to be the same
Men I'm surrounded by, these
Men are here, as vivid as
Plasma, these men are
Fatherless like myself,
Some blind, most hateful,
Majority of them ignorant,
These men

REFLECTION OF MAN

The reflection of a man, Utopia
Wright here standing
With my chest
Pressed firm to
The wall, stripped
Search for contraband,
Frisked and
Spat on, tortured for my words,
Loved for the same,
like me, love me,
Fight back, free
The ones deserving,
 I'm living proof
Of something to someone,
whatever that may be,
I take that title with
No problem

TUESDAY MORNING

Standing behind the thin
Line between prison
And freedom, a deep
Session of therapeutic
Evaluation of the mind,
Where all the horror
Is stored, placed inside,
Only to perform in front
Of a population of
Men I hate, all the signs
Of a criminal is present,
All the characteristics
Of a murderer has been
Classified, sealed
Tight is my case,
I'm here for long, Life
Without the possibility
Of ever seeing you again
And it's only Tuesday Morning

MANCHESTER PEARL

A collection of young black,
Males talking that talk,
Walking that walk, New York
City's finest, Brooklyn
To the Bay area, we
All wear the same pain
In our faces, races and
Images of difference
Means nothing, police see
The hate clearly, they hate
The fact that I'm me,
Yet this is their chosen
Profession,
No beefing with that, I am
The first criminal redefined by
The old school division,
Used to calculate the time given,
Thank you your honor for
The opportunity,
I've grown to know your daughter,
She visits and writes on
A regular basis and I haven't
Even tasted it, I am who
They paint me as,
Utopia Wright, better known
To some as
Manchester Pearl,
Aqua, The Big Fish

A DREAMER

The disposition of Utopia Wright, a therapy from
Boredom and silence, the whisper of nothing bothers me
Most, outside of my mind is where I contain the
Sadness, when the lights darken and the hollering
Begins, I prepare for the tears, deeply soaked in
A pillow as hard as the gavel's flames after
Sentencing, summer through winter
I'm sad, so stressed,
Uncomfortable with my current situation,
The idea of living life continues to fade,
As I fade to the next page
Of my disposition, I often think of you

INGERSOL HOUSES

Forever lost in the
Eyes of my
Mother,
Who loved
Me without
A thought,
She moved on
To bigger and
Better things,
A place fit for
Kings and Queens,
A far cry from the
Housing projects
Where we both
Found love, where
Gloria and I
First made love,
Where she
Met my father
Charles and kept
Him a secret
As long as she
Lived, I cried
Many years for
That hurt most,
Yet I remained
Focused and
Filled with love
Knowing It was all

STICKINESS

Missing my wife and children
who I love most, furthermore
Praise them for their
Dedication to
My current situation,
I pretend to be
Someone they once knew,
Unable to show them
The changes
Made over the years,
The endless acts
Of violence towards
Police and fellow
Inmates, I'd hate for
Them to witness me
In such rage, it would
Hurt to project to them the
Beast they assumed would
Become of me because
That is not the man I am

EVERYSTEP

The one thing I don't need is
More blood on my hands, more
Voices to silence me to sleep, more
Mourning and regret I do not need,
later in life you will see the remorse
Displayed on a daily basis, I'm trying to
Become a man, trying to regroup and allow
Myself to love, it's not easy, especially
When surrounded by the world's most
Ignorant individuals, with an everyday complex,
I am Utopia Wright, loving every step

KIAMESHA WRIGHT

Shower me with
The love of my mother,
Who I miss most,
Her time cut short
By madness, pure
Havoc how a life so
Appreciated was taken
In the first leg
Of this race indicated
As life, sometime
In the near future
We will be together
To rekindle a time
Lost and friendship
Misplaced, may you rest with
The rest of God's angels
And watch over your
Youngest child with good
Intentions of cleansing my soul
from demonic thought

DAILY NEWS

Speak loud
When spoken to, these
Men only hear a whisper
Of the truth, they will
Never understand where
I'm coming from, not even
My mother quite got me,
May she rest, These days
Are slowly bringing me down
I'm not even writing
As much as I should,
This pen feels funny
In my left hand,
If only I had my right,
Unfortunately it
Was broken on a man's
Face, from the depths of jail
To the hollow hallways of
The projects,
I still represent the struggle,
I'm still on top of my vices,
Still praying for the lost,
while hoping one day it will
All come together

COURTESY, PROFESSIONALISM, RE-SPECT

These liars, bleed
Deadly deaths, I pray
Your soul rest in
The paws of hell,
I hope your children
See the pain in your eyes
When you tell them how
You killed a man today,
How you beat a man to death,
How you spat in his face
And pissed on his chest,
I hope they see the truth in
Your eyes, the monstrous thoughts
of molestation that defines you,
The overall picture according to you,
Your wicked ways will reveal truth
And my words will continue
Long after your kids become
Adults and long after you
And your friends kill me,
Bastards

O

What I want to say
I can't, my words
Are being monitored
For gang activity
I live for myself,
A one man gang at best,
Stand alone, die alone
From Brooklyn to
Sullivan, I am
Utopia Wright,
Shackles and all
I'm believed to be
A problem for
This facility, they
Can blow me, early
I awake to an aroma
Of self pity,
A Hard-on and morons,
I'm surrounded by dicks,
Pause, for time here
Is shared with good
People I consider friends,
Because when my life
Is on the line
These men wont fold
Nor bend, if you label
That a gang, then
It is what it is, unfortunately

REACH

Truthfully speaking, each child
Needs attention and me being in prison
Helps not a bit, as I sit and watch
Nothing beautifying pass before my eyes,
I'm forced to wonder whether life will
Ever be the same, a bitch isn't it?
Something to think about for the rest
Of my life, doing time, a swallow of hurt,
Remorse and guilt, sentenced to second guess
My own morals, something so discouraging
It's sickening, a feeling so silencing
It burns flesh, nevertheless change has badly
Taken over and if I stay here any longer,
I will never be the same

UNEMOTIONAL

locked in for hours,
I beat a drum with
My bare hands,
A melody heard through
The facility as a sign
Of relief, waiting
for a release,
If ever, just the
same ole me,
Representing my
children through
The eyes of my God,
As the many eyes
Eat away at my skin
I write again the
Disposition of
A man battling
The coming
of age theory,
The time
Given to endure all
Life's lesson has
Never felt so depressing,
Missing my mother,
Whose bones are buried
In a cemetery I've
Never seen in my life,
Her soul laid to rest
In an utopia,

SAGE

Under me sleeps a man, foul
In all ways, a loser with
No morals or sprit,
A monster without
Guidance or remorse,
A savage or some sort of
Beast who wishes death
To all man, woman and child,
An attitude I've never seen on
A man, his determination
To kill overwhelms me,
His dedication to death is tragic,
He sleeps loudly below, as I write above

RAPTURE

The secret lives of
The monstrous
Men who prey on
Single white females,
Living single on
The Upper East Side,
Lurking in vestibules and
Subway stations
Alike, day or night
They strike their
Victims cowardly, from
Behind, changing the
Outcome of a woman's
Life forever,
The masked rapist
From hell will
Always strike again,
Leaving his victims
In pure panic, lost
And reminded of
What was forcefully taken

SUNDAY SCHOOL

I once shared time with the son of a preacher who murdered
His father, during Sunday morning service, in front of the
whole church, stabbing him eight times in The chest, now the
son of a preacher parades his Islamic colors without end, he
is Now extremely confident of his spot in heaven because his
new way of life has Become a release to an uncontrollable
life of being a Christian

"In war, truth is the first casualty."

— **Aeschylus**

NEW BORN

A new birth to inhale
Life for its principles and
Not for what it's worth,
Yet asking is it worth
The time invested or is life as
Meaningless as it gets,
Nevertheless, every awaking night
I'm reminded of my crime,
Not by time, but by the voice of
My victim, through dreams and echoes,
Shouting to me, his last cry of
"don't shoot"

MURDERER

A man informed me of a murder,
To take place in three days,
He asked if I would participate,
My response to him was "no thanks."
Plus the reason for the
Man to be killed was petty,
I saw in his eyes that
My response bothered him,
So he applied pressure
To his voice and threatened
My life, little did he
Understand another threat,
Means nothing, when
Death only brings relief,
In other words, fuck him.
I'm here for good,
My words flew at him fierce
Enough that he didn't reply,
He didn't sigh or utter a peep,
However, three days later that same man
Plotting a murder was stabbed
Seventeen times in his
Sleep And I had nothing
To do with it,
I promise

THE SAGA

When these lights darken, the
Hollering begins, often I'm
Lost in a book
Preparing for my death,
At best, I awake
Only to be counted
Like a herd of sheep,
As these bastards
Scream at my face their hatred,
I plant my feet firm,
Head straight ahead,
Staring into the
Hell mouth of man,
Speaking, withholding nothing,
My disposition continues,
Without pause

LINEN STREETS

I was expected to value wrongdoing
And cater to the bosom of crime,
Like a child clinging to life,
A frontal view of poverty exposed
By an illusion of money and woman,
A prepaid existence to life in prison,
For years I tried to separate the beast from
The man within, a true win/win in the endless
Game against crime and all the exposure it's getting

ETHICAL BALANCE

During my day
I bought properties with my
Jewish partner
And we had an understanding
On how money would be split,
After my arrest I learned
A hard lesson in the game of
Business, but that's okay,
However my son is in a wheelchair
And my daughter's mind is slipping,
Not to mention my wife Is stripping
To feed her addiction to sex, but who am
I to Complain about money,
Friends and family, when hard times
Spare no child, woman or man

DADDY'S LITTLE EVERYTHING

My desire for
Children overwhelmed
Most women, the challenge of
Motherhood, froze many in their
Steps, which brings me to
Gloria's first-born child,
The pleasantness on her face
Was expressionless, no words could
Describe such determination and pride,
Unless of course you were speaking
Of my darling daughter, who
Became an instant mint in my eyes
Yet to no surprise she would grow
To envy her mother and the things
She preached, unavoidable estrogen
Clashes, a battle of the bosom,
As I would say, yet missing them all
Yesterday as much as today

PETTY CASH

A friend of mine
Killed himself, two
Hours after his first
Born was introduced to the world,
A sight missed by a man focused on
Money, sought in the alleyways
And dead end's life led
Him to believe was the only way
To get his hands on what hardworking
Folks consider petty cash

JAKE

I prayed for
Him twice, as the
Fiesta next door lasted
Until the early
Morning, It left
Me sick in the stomach to
Hear the abuse of another
Man, that's life, better
Him than me, I live for
My own problems,
Sins and prayers, I feel no
Remorse for any man here

ONCE AGAIN

Literally he sleeps
Above me in a
Temporary daze of
Freedom, in
His state of dream, he
Hugs his loved ones
Once again, missing
Everything about
Their lives, he begs to his
God for another chance at life,
Only to awake to An outcome
Controlled by the state,
He wakes to take a shit,
Leaving behind an odor as
Foul as the system that has
Sentenced him, wanting to
Dream more, he returns to his bunk
To a dream where he and
His wife make love, once again

JOURNEY WRIGHT

I wonder if they even notice
My daughter's dedication to peace and
How blessed she is to be mentally raised by a man
With the same face as her big brother,
Who she loves most, I Love my daughter
For all the words said and written
Because through it all she continues to
Inform the lost of her father, who's doing
Life without handouts or cooperation
From anyone, unaware
Of his manhood and struggle

PREY

My mother heard it all from her
Bedroom door, an abuse so
Raw, it was far from comical, an
Experience so discouraging it was
More than enough because it
Was I, who fought off his sexual
Advances every chance I could,
But on some nights he
Penetrated me deeper than
Where he put his penis,
He mistook me for a
Woman, therefore forgiveness
Could never refill
What has been taken from
My childhood because
Now suffering moves me more
Than anything else

TIMELESS ENCORE

My mother was honestly
Fair, not worthy of
The tragic outcome of her life,
A child's champion, molded
To monitor my decisions in life,
To provide and shelter my family
With her presence and time,
All in all she was a
Stand-up gal, loving of
The small things, overlooked by
The hard times Brought
Forth with time

PERFECT ATTENDANCE

A life
Sentence reminds him
Of where he's from
And where he hasn't been
In the past ten years,
All he knows is this place,
Even still he smiles, sincere
And smooth, motivating actually, kind of
Makes me want to do right,
His belief system in religion is limited,
Being the man I am I slide information
His way, hoping one day we could
Build a system, bulletproof from
Police and fellow inmates
Who hate positive motivation,
A revolution of some sort,
Just a thought, I'm full of those

DEMANDING

It's so hard walking a straight line,
When knowing survival here, is at
Its weakest, surrounded by the devil,
Controlling the ignorance is obsolete,
Juggling two lives, of a married man
With children, while the other half
Is a Pitiful sight, the two identities of
Man walking closer to the gates,
I pause, continue, then reflect, time
Has changed me, time has killed me,
Time is all I know

UNIFORMED

Blessed to be me, another moment seized
Beyond the wall, rested safely in
The belly of the beast, the rest will be relieved
To know I'm present, forever stuck in
This permanent state, in custody of the state
Of New York, can't begin to express the sorrow
Felt deep inside my chest, a feeling of remorse
Will forever be, my victim's eyes makes this clear, yet
Faith in my God keeps me afloat, knowing He'll save
My soul from the intended hands of hell, I hope,
Because the rest of my life is a period, I am Utopia,
Founder of love, original man, born black
In the Borough of Brooklyn

THE NATION

I can feel it, So hot to touch
It burns, my palms stuck
On empty, yet still the devil
Begs me to rejoin him and keep
The violence popular,
I refused, for God knows my soul
Better than those I hold close,
Producing a feeling of heavy misery,
Pure pain, I'm forced to let rage
Express its purpose, 85 percent
Of my time spent avoiding
These temptations, I am nothing
But man, they speak in tongues
Understood by myself
As devil music, speaking
In tunes of sins, I begin
To cautiously walk,
Only to be confronted
By the savage of man

DEAR RAHSON

Abort the current page,
 Beginning a new chapter in
life, as long as I'm able
To write these words,
My children will have a father,
With my disposition being
The only lifeline left,
I trust in you, my friend,
To convert my thoughts
Into text, keep providing
The writing material and I'll
Make sure to convey to
You my disposition,
Keep me in your prayers
And I'll do the same,
 Always keep God first and
Take care of yourself

TAKE HEED

Observing the savage
Folk of an inner circle, of
Mostly Negroes and
Spanish men who kill
For fun, hate for glory,
Pride and religion,
Subjectively forbidden to
Channel any real thoughts,
If God is watching
His children,
Like many believe, then
These monsters will have
Their day to be judged,
Indeed

"We survived slavery because we held onto one another. The moment we found independence, we began to commit suicide."

— Dr. Tesehloane Keto

SITTING STILL

Sitting here, four walls to my death, a voice
Plays over and over, blinding are the walls,
Wanting more, hating myself, smoking cigarettes
Without hesitation, anger builds, "silence kills" written
On the ceiling, no escaping this, acceptance has set,
Eager for death, the sound of nothing appears, an echo
Of nostalgia, a reoccurrence of a feeling I can't quite
Measure, doing time in November, sitting still forever

ORINGINAL MESSAGE

Through my travels
I've seen the likes of
All savage beings,
From hell, they sprout
Like wild thorns, stinging
Tragedy in the lives
Of God's children,
Never to witness such
Horrific images is a privilege,
For love is limited to just
A sexual touch,
No feelings or emotions
Allowed, translated or
Formed, leaving those
Thoughtful and beautiful,
Lost without love,
Therefore without hope

JUSTIFIED

Struggling with pride, suffering with life,
Justified by reason Of insanity, hurting
Inside, outside lives a lie, what's seen
Is a mirror image of a fake, a liar of
All sorts, tolerance plays a big part
In the misrepresentation, faced with
Issues of an unsecured future,
So beautiful, I scream, so mean, I lean
Forward, pressing my hands properly against
My chest, hoping my heart beat never skips,
Yet plays continuously, repeat after repeat

FASTING

Unaware
Of his surroundings, he
Took his eye off the ball,
Landing face first in
The hands of
Vicious man handlers,
Preying the night's sleep,
Their creep is mean,
Ice cold, nothing
Unfamiliar about their hunger,
A situation all must
Endure, yet this place
Is the last place,
I'd want to
Swallow the sword

GET A GRIP

Ignoring men whose ignorance
Sells volumes, forming a shield from
Those who settle, keeps me available
To pick and choose who's worthy of my time,
For it's too precious to be wasted on the latest
Trend, I'm more than annoyed at those
Having nothing much to say,
Therefore, their words blow by without
Acknowledgement

HOMOCIDE

The price paid for murder is
Incalculable, when most were
Unable to witness a murderer,
Murdered by a murderer after
Witnessing murder, through the eyes
Of a murderer

PURPLE HEARTED

I'm not the man I was
Ten years ago,
Time has made that clear,
My only fear is for the lives
Of my children, as I pray never a day,
Would they spend a second in
Such a place like this,
Utopia Wright, a man, a husband,
A father to most,
Walking a path pre designed,
Preaching in a fashion Christ
Intended, my position in the system
Has never been questioned,
My disposition will never end

THE PSALMS OF MAN

The distance between lies and greed, spread thin,
Blending in to be cool put a lot of good men behind the
Fence, forever surrounded by the coolest, toughest men
In the state of New York, just another moment
In the life of Utopia, still a man, placed in the
System to make crucial decisions,
options are avail, no Denying that fact,
However most can not help but do the
Things they do, society paints this one picture
Of your average inner city man,
that being the image of Violence,
adultery and laziness, hard times
presents itself In many forms,
hungriness seemingly is the
number one killer, leaving it to
this one man to take care of a family
Of seven, working in
the stock room, at Duane Reade, is not
Cutting it, so taking what's needed is genius because
For a man to sit back and wait for another man,
To provide for his family, is borderline foolery

ENTER 1997

Lusting more now
Than ever, wanting the juices
And comfort of my wife, the same
Woman who loves to love not loving me,
A bullshit theory on life I wish
She'd reconsider, yet her loving is
Worth the time spent in
The hole, heatedly stimulated, I
Squeeze off a batch to Gloria's eyes,
As she rides me to a sober sleep,
I awake to a new year, a new day,
Yet the same shit

SUMMER SANCHEZ

I'm losing my stripes,
Following this one around,
Wondering if any of her time is
Spent with me on her mind,
A feeling I wish to escape,
However the reality is this,
I'm falling in love with
The theory, that this
Woman can provide me
With something my wife
Can not, will not and won't,
I'm all alone on this one,
She's sassy and sexy,
At best erotic with her simple
Arousal, a drifter by choice,
She's never around to
Hear my cries, she's always
On the go from here to
There, living her life,
Not once taking the
Time to acknowledge the
Feelings I'm desperately
Trying to present before
Her beautifying eyes,

MY CELLIE

Awkward in stance, his glance showed
Me his motives in one setting, hard as
Time for the youth, the truth
Was found in his eyes which told a story,
In a tongue unfamiliar to my own, one hundred
And one reasons why I killed him, now I'm reminded
Once a day why I shouldn't have

NUDE

Banging these dudes faces into walls, before
Dawn, my sex drive grows uncontrollable, a desire
Aborted by the time received, a focus on lovemaking
Is beautiful to some, as for me I rest
Hard with my balls released for any man
Who's thinking sexual, them fools will never
Get a chance to relax, anal alert from a far,
A gasp or sigh for help never entered one's mind,
Now forever taken and violated, I lay
Awaken to the smell of sexual frustration

ONE MAN SHOW

The smell of men feeds off a certain foul odor that rests sharply on the tip Of one's nose, although time freezes For the many with release dates, I'm unable to relate, my Way of thinking is far from that of the free or those on Their Way home to their loved ones, blessed and all after Nine Years in, I'm still not fully understanding the Situation I've been placed in, it seems like a dream on Some days, a role of some sort with me as the lead Character in a one man play entitled

"The Disposition Of Utopia Wright"

KARMA (FULL CIRCLE)

The truth explains
A lot of the lies I shied
From as a youth, walking
Tall with them Brooklyn boys,
Who I knew for sure would
Always support my violent
Misadventures, each side,
Of the South and Eastside of
The projects, was my homeland,
A security provided by my
Brothers and cousins who
Paved the way for the cycle
To continue, as my generation
Of gangsters stepped up to the
Plate, my life was written years
Before I was sentenced to life,
It's the blood in the streets
That made this so,
But who am I to complain?
I'm just a man doing time,
Watching my life slip
Through, to a place I've always
Considered to be Hell

BREAKING LAWS

Bending over for no man,
A sexual desire for some,
So nasty to speak of, the thought
Of another, other than a woman,
Pretending for what, my balls
Stay close with the package
Given by God, bone in the morning,
Just is what it is, nothing
I can do about that, matter of fact,
She is the one I lust for,
Her pictures do more
Than one might imagine,
Only a man with discipline can
Relate, the time served proves
Why I'm me, the many years inside shows
Why my chest is poking out
And my back seems to be as solid as
Rock, a workout determined
By the dedication to discipline,
The only way I know how to live

SAVED

The choice
Of wanting and feeling
Clashes, forming a communication
 Between two that should never
Be tampered, loving someone beside
Yourself, besides family, whose
Love for you is one sided, unevenly
Cared for by the many men and women
Walking God's green earth
Searching for a friend or lover
To complain about, just the small
Things lovers encounter during
Their greatest moments in life,
A lovers best friend should be
A lovers best friend, at best a
Lover should be one who
Loves without a thought or
Probable cause

KISS AND TELL

How could life become so intolerable,
From terrible two's to horrible, so hateful
I black out, suffering from
Something I can't put my finger on,
But I let the words flow, leave me alone
And watch me transform your last
Word into my next, sit back and let
Time escape the air and I'll fill
A blank paper with my life and watch you
React in a manner I'd already expected,
Unfortunate men tend to understand,
Woman who love understand the words
Used, I believe you most, the women
Of my life never knew me well,
Never would they take the time
Used to get used to me,
Unless the woman in question
Was the glorious Gloria Wright,
A beautiful woman placed In
My life for reasons I'd rather
Not express, yet believe she
Is and will always be the one
Understanding of my disposition

CONSENSUAL

A lonely mother
With no one to touch, a body
Deserving of love, a man wanting
To provide that affection,
Standing between us are
These bars and gates, a couple
Of guards and a life sentence,
Stay with me and I promise,
One day we will become one,
Lusting each other into
A lovers reunion, Gloria and
Utopia, man and woman both in
Need of passion lost

IT'S MORNING

Her appetite for life is envied,
She makes me want to love her,
She is the foundation
Of this generation of children,
I intend to raise, her soul
Will never be compared,
She belongs to me, She loves
The taste of my skin, it
Reminds her of candy, sweet
To taste, she will never
Want to hurt me, why would she?
She will always lay
Beside me, fighting beside her man,
The battles between man and I,
For all we got is us, as
We lay without conscious thoughts
Of today nor tomorrow,
It's already morning

NO CURSING

He wouldn't stop the
Talking, couldn't keep
His thoughts to himself,
Selfish of him to ask
For my toothpaste,
This man is a bastard
Of all men, determined to
Lie his way to death,
As morning sets, just he
And I remain, stained teeth
And bad breath, the new
Day brings more of the same
Bullshit and regrets

WANTED

Holding hands,
A romance pure and
Free of argument,
Tailored garments,
Catered food and
Family, a marriage
Of two of the worlds
Greatest, a song to
The newlyweds, heard
By the city's rush,
Who would have thought
These two would marry?
Yet they did, without question
Or doubt, love played its part
In the making of a family,
Of this man and this woman

COMPETETION

I'm only man, flesh
Of flesh, born black
To a tar, yet I'm expected
To compete with the many
Men, whose faces reflect
Mine, at times the competition
Is scarce, however something
Simple as a stare can raise
The rivalry level to life or death,
Making my life that much harder,
Similar to the relationship
Between me and my father,
I'm trying to find him
Before death finds me,
A competition worth
The fight, a goal worth
The struggle, an ambition
Worth the time, my days
Consist of a life long
Competition between a
Father and child, yet through
The eyes of a champion,
I'm well prepared for the ride

"Imagination is more important than knowledge."

— Albert Einstein

IMAGINE

An imagination so vivid, a
Vision misunderstood,
By the man hovering above
Her naked body, so much
Disgust, she allows him
To finish his lusting, now
So stubborn she moves
On to his friends, as they too
Do things to her body that
She doesn't remember giving
Consent for, love making so
Rough and forced her vagina bleeds,
In desperation she awakes to
Another, him being the one she
Came to visit, slowly falling
Back to a state of dream,
She continues her imagination
Process without end

UNDERSTANDING

I could never get back
The times lost, you and I
Wanting more of the same
Shit everyone else endured,
The sleepless nights, brought forth
From endless nights of fighting,
Blame it on the rain, a classic
Tale of two, You and I, as
Close to another as the next,
A token of affection found in
The eyes of each other,
A time hurried by goodbyes
And so longs, a hurt felt daily,
A dream slept through and through,
The life and times of me wouldn't be
Shit without the life and times of you

CRISP

Sounding the words
Out to hear what's been
Said, some ten years prior
To the day of my first
Child's introduction to
The world of Fort Greene
Brooklyn, these same words,
Misheard by the many who
Wished death to me and mine,
Words spat in the faces of
Two parents trying to make
The best out of such a hard
Situation, words so violent and
Unforgivable that it hurts
To relive the time, just a reminder
Of the days of ole, wishing mostly
That those days were now
Because these days are harder
Than ever

SUNDAY MORNING

Nothing to do, another
Endless battle between man
And me, the freedom I once
Craved, has grown to pass, lonely
Times ahead gets me down,
Seemingly depressed over
A love life now void, a father
Of two, husband to none, a
Question mark worth all
The many questions asked,
Upon realization, I awoke
To the smell of self pity,
Shallow and degrading, I
fall back into a state
Of regret

JUST BECAUSE

I inked some words
I'd wish to explain to my family,
Swollen hands keeps me from
Writing the words said,
From the beginning of time
To time served, I'm sorely
Emotionally fucked, the mind
Is losing an endless battle,
These days appear as they
Always did, the same shit
All hours on end, the blue
Sky explains a different tale
Of life, lights out for the few
Living positive in such
Horrible conditions, I
Hope you men win the
Battle for I'm completely
Out of sprit, meaning
I'm basically out of time

ACCESS STOLEN

Give me free speech
And free all the many
Men, losing their lives
Behind the wall of death,
Give me the truth
And keep the lies
To yourselves, for
I'm in desperate need
Of change, give me the
Maximum amount of respect
And lose the attitude
That follows that
New ego you've discovered,
And I'll give you
The words of my
Life without pause,
Haste or pretend

SEVEN MILES A DAY

Whenever opportunity
Presents itself, I write
The words that comes
Natural, not Dictionary
Defined, yet simply my
Disposition in life,
The average day comes
And goes, I'm just doing
Time, watching life squeeze
The mercy out of my mind,
A criminal I am not,
However since my
Arrival here, I have become
More violent in
Mind body and soul,
If I wasn't who
My mother intended
Me to be, then I must
Be my older brother's
Least favorite person,
He never comes
To visit nor does he
Write, I take it
I'm a failure of some sort,
But I'm just like him, a good
Person in love with
His wife, yet in a split
Second, I took a life,
Call it what you want

A TASTE

The bleach, thrown in her face,
Was a sign of love, crazy as it seems
I'm very proud to admit the loveless ness
Missed, the love once provoked, a winners love,
A signature line of lovely days to come,
With loving on the mind I'm leaving your love life
Left up to you, loving me more means
Loving to love all those in which I love,
A parable to a life seen, from
The opposite side of the tasteless
Lovers of your past, future and present

OTHERWISE

The Criminal they see,
Is that of a man who
Walked during the days
Of depression, the days
Of money and woman scarce,
And afraid of the next day,
Not knowing where the food
Is coming from, they'll rather
Shoot you for a meal, to live
Longer than their kids, the
Selfish mind of man,
The wicked ways of the
Hungry, the world will
Never quite grasp this
Issue, shaking in one's
Bones are the old, former
Hustlers of their day,
Stopping at nowhere to
Keep hope alive, feeding
On the innocence to
Continue walking a path,
Full of food and money

WALL STREET

Throughout the Bronx,
I see problems between Hispanics
And blacks, awkward I forward
Back to the issues at
Hand, the man in the mirror
Never seen life clearer,
However I'm never happy
With my current situation,
They hate the fact that I'm black,
I hate the fact that they care,
I figured time would have changed
The indifferences between them
And I, what a lie, I'm the blackest
Man walking this corner,
Always wondering if
My life is actually in danger,
I laughed and moved on towards the
Corner store, next thing I
Did was run back upstairs,
Grabbed my pistol, kissed my mother,
Inhaled long and Paused

AGONIZED

Bring it, more violence,
More rage to let out,
The monster inside
Thrives on the weak,
Speaking of the soft,
Incapable and fragile,
I'm a beast for the money,
The hunger comes first,
As God walks close,
My victim sleeps,
Only to wake to
The wrath of a problem
Child, frozen in a space
As tiny as a bathroom,
The silence overwhelms
The positivity, leaving the
Unknown vulnerable to
Death, the activity of living
Ten years in this hell
Shows clearly I'm not the man I
Once was, many have been fortunate
To walk away, while others
Rest In peace for an entire
Adulthood in prison,
No wonder the world
Revolves the way it does
And the children suffer
The most from the crimes
People play

"God gives every bird its food, but He does not throw it into its nest."

– J.G. Holland

AS WE LAY

Its morning, as we lay,
A man's wife sits in worry,
Her hubby, dipping
In other women,
The finest flock
Of dimes, sharing
Time with each race,
Their faces differ in shade,
Yet sex drives remain
In neutral, truly
Ruling out charm
As an influence,
Explosive sex, proven
Signs of fulfillment,
Hospitalized for
Guilty pleasures
Entertained in the
Night, for my mother's
Sake, I protect
Sickness from
Family, sexual
Fantasies defines me,
As we lay

WANTING

I love her so much,
She's just what I asked
For, I prayed for her
And there she appeared,
It took three years before
I gathered the balls
To approach,
Until that day I was
Mere mortal, walking
High on life, never
Understanding the
Power of woman,
Yet fighting the lust
Of man, she stands closer to
Me now, more than ever,
It's my time to savor
The moment and press
Forward my example
Of a real man, she
Gladly replied yes
And I left with a
Phone number in hand,
A chest full of pride
And the confidence
Of a new man

DEATH CALLED

Why the sudden pain
After so many years
Of good fortune,
Now the thought of
Killing myself crosses
My mind, at first I
Brushed it off,
Telling myself I'm
Too blessed to be stressed,
Yet after years of hurt,
I'm ready to depart this
Earth, leaving behind
All things beautiful
And with meaning, if
Only I could find my
True purpose for staying,
If the signs from my
God was visible I'd
Stay here and continue,
But nothing seems real
Anymore, everything
Is fuzzy and I want out

DEMONIC

Borderline fake and wicked
Men want me to kill, the thrill
Of hate pokes fun at me,
The voices of Satan transmits clear,
He awaits my arrival with
Ease, certain of my death,
He smiles, his goons spit
At me flames of racism,
I inhale it all, wanting to become
Like them, I sold my
Goals and dream for a taste,
Only to receive a forty ounce
Of madness in the form
Of blood, drenched in a
Liquid unknown, I finally
Get to meet my maker

DESTINATION UNCERTAIN

Walking closer to the gates of hell,
Unaware of the outcome,
Standing closer to the piers
Of heaven's waters,
Never to regret the message
Left by the man in the mirror,
Walking behind the danger of
A players last call for whores,
At least ten million will lie
To each other and miss the bus
Headed uptown, where the people
Are awaiting your arrival in peace

FATHERLESS PRIDE

If anybody asks, I'm
Never to be interrupted
And when your mother
Comes home, I'm not to be
Bothered, if the super
Knocks on the door,
You don't know where
Your father is,
And by the time I wake up,
You better be finished
Cleaning the apartment
And don't try to be slick by
Sweeping dirt under the carpet,
Now as for your mother, well
I'll take care of her when she gets
Home, If you need any money, look
Inside the drawer by the phone
Now, give your daddy a kiss
Because Lord knows I love you
And if anybody asks about your
Father, remember what I told you

GLORIA'S BLUES

The sky hovers the
Sun like a mother to a child
Or a child to milk,
I was built for this
Type of situation
An adaptation
From the streets
To prison, nothing
Missing, but God's
Word and with that said,
May you bring the light
Back into my life
And open the gates for
Your youngest boy
Utopia, if Gloria
Only knew the pain
She's delivering to
Our children, for they
Know no better than
Mommy and Daddy,
The last of my loved ones
Shouldn't be left without
A mother's guidance,
However, may you
Send her this message
Through divine intervention
And I'll continue to pray
For me, her and our two children

HOLDING BACK

All my life I've
Been losing,
So sore, I struggle
To keep pace,
Humorous, the
Thought of a win
Win situation followed
By my first and last
Name, no doubt
I've been beaten
Many times over,
Broken down to the
Core, stripped of reason,
Dreaming of better days,
Until one day she appeared,
Slowly we discovered a love
For one another, suddenly
I've been winning
Ever since, endlessly

HUGS N KISSES

Brushed off only
To be ignored and placed
Last, on a long list
Of bitches my wife wishes
Was me, her new way of
Life is now loving women
With the same tongue used to
Moisten me with, the same
Insides I'd kill to return to,
A mistake made now has her
Licking things she always
Claimed she'd never, how clever
Is this woman I love most,
How inconsiderate this bitch,
To keep me in the dark
On issues that may or
May not concern her husband,
Yet what the
Fuck can I do about that from
Behind the fence

TODAY

I killed a man,
Nothing more to
Regret or feel sorrow
For, it was I who on
That day pulled the
Trigger and let go
The most horrible
Demon inside,
As I waited for the law,
I saw my life flash
Before my eyes,
Never again will I
See freedom
Or feel the insides
Of my wife, nor
Would I see my kids'
Dreams come true
Before my eyes,
So young, yet so
Mature, they smile
When all I can do is cry,
Locked in, a struggle within
Itself, my preparation
For death is in the air,
Today

VINTAGE TIMES SQUARE

A moisture of nostalgia,
Her insides are pure,
Standard positioning,
Nothing more than a motion
Of in and out, a mist of
Arousal scented by
A collage of kisses,
A collection of Barry White,
To settle the mood,
An emotion of force
Makes it harder to stop
Penetrating
Her sexual press,
Energetic in oral
Presentation, she swallows
My pride in whole,
Leaving me escaped
For the longest
Eight seconds of my life,
I wept and prayed to my God,
For this feeling of
Pleasure never to depart
And within a flash
It was over and
I awoke to my right
Hand dripping
With would
Be children

HAPPY MOTHER'S DAY

The day she passed
You stepped up and allowed a teenager
To be just that, instilling the basic
Things needed for a life uncertain,
Such importance played a big
Part in the man I am today,
With all praises sent my way
From a precious angel
Of all sorts, dedicated to
Her children, her children's
Children and all those
Which she loves, my favorite
Person when talking about
Who I love, she is who I
Intend to be, a founder of
Family life, a mission we
All must understand is not
As easy as it seems,
God bless this woman,
For she has raised
A man understanding
Of struggle and adversity,
With that said, I love you
Most and happy Mothers day

"Freedom is the only solution to an endless battle between man and me, for man is the only thing standing between me and my freedom."

– Utopia Wright

THROUGH THE WIRE

I'm lost in the cycle
Of wondering if I'll
Ever see the beautiful
Gloria Wright, never
Again should I want another
Woman, Gloria is to be the last
One living who actually cares
About me, maybe not, because
Her behavior paints another
Story, feelings of worry
Keeps me focused on
What needs to be done,
However time has separated
Me from my children, therefore
God bless them and no
On else

REMARKABLE TIMING

Certain circumstances
Branch into problems,
Better known as issues,
Wondering if love
Could hold us together
Or whether we measured
The baking soda properly
Or will we lose profit,
Playing a game that killed
So many before us, Jesus
Hovers the cross, unaware
Of his death, we kneel to pray,
Spirituality unseen by the
Hearts of man, struggle versus
Religion, a game dangerous
If you let it, freedom to all
God's prophets awaiting
My arrival in the end

MEANING

Meaning, a term
Hazardous to lifers,
A present day
Default similar to
A drunken monkey
Dancing in place,
A nappy head Negro
Child looking up to the
Gangsters of a generation
Ahead of his own, summer
Time hook ups with as many
Women as one man can, sharing
Their snatch with friends and
Family, meaning she gets
Around, she loves it,
A daddy to them broads,
They need me, bitches
For sale, another topic
Altogether, I mean
I smoke weed, drink my
Jailhouse hooch, home
Grown for the world to
Understand my reason
For being, meaning I'm
Loved by many, meaning
I'm only flesh, meaning
I'm only human

SOLUTIONS

My favorite person
Is living with a sickness,
That has cursed my
Loved ones for too
Many years, the will of
This person is beautiful,
At times I cry deep, the
Thought of it all hurts most,
On days it becomes over bearing,
Sending me into rage of
Hate for those who made
This possible, my favorite person,
Who wants so much more, has
To be limited to wherever
Time allows him to roam,
A trace unseen, a simple
Duty of sacrifice and
Compromise has passed
Before my eyes, now
I truly understand
That I was put here to
Live for, those unable to
Live freely, I stand for
All things missed and
All words cherished,
I am your favorite person
Too, it's written all over
Your face, Thanks again
For the time baby boy,
I love you

SUNSHINE PRATT

Desperately she massages
My chest with her tongue,
Up and down soothing to
A touch of pleasantness,
Both excited by the thought
Of lovemaking, we became one,
Collapsed on a bed spread
Eagle in all directions, wetness
And erections blinding the
Truth of the matter, she
Belongs to another and Gloria
Is mine, she needs to be held,
Her being the woman placed
Properly on top of my shaft,
Another day to suck her nipples
Will assure me another night
On the couch, another risk worth
Taking, why not?
She's explosive in oral,
A pleasure unmatched by
The many before her, time
Will definitely determine
When it will come to an end,
Until then, I'm in it for
The minute

DEATH OF A CHAMPION

The look in the eyes of my daughter,
When she saw me for the first
Time in seven years, the tears
Began early, a sign of love missed,
Nothing funny about the pain
Felt, she melted me, a feeling
So sour, I can't move forward,
It hurts so bad, her eyes told
The story of Gloria, all the things
She's done in the past showed
Clearly through Journey's mannerism
And body language, I walked
Away from her visit with
No spirit, if death was an option,
I'd give in, so sad how my life
Effects so many I love,
Yet I stand strong, a champion
In my own, a solider in my own
War against man, it begins with
Me, a form of greatness only found
In the heart of man, the only man
Who actually cares, me, myself the
Only man worth giving another
Chance, yet I'm not the man my
Family can rely on, not the man
Who they can depend on for the
Things needed now, therefore
I am who I am, I am the man these
Prison walls created

TRANSEXUAL THOUGHTS

Woman, man
Never could compare to such
Pleasure found between the
Thighs of God's most precious,
The woman, a treasure seen
By the many men walking the
Tier, a gangster's vice, many
Men are here for the killings of
Woman, whether killed or killed for,
It's all about the woman, if properly
Controlled, a woman could run this
World with just her touch, my
Woman will tell you the same, another
Day to kiss mine, I'd kill and sacrifice a lot of
My possession for a taste of her soft lips,
A razor to the face of the
Soft, fragile and frail men walking
This tier, with a different perception
Of what a woman is

SEVEN

Born again, the real of
The fake, strong in history,
Living it daily, making it with
Words written, in all forms
Of using the same words,
Different days brings different
Titles, emotions and pain,
Humping around no more,
My penis is stiffly placed
In my greens, ask about me,
Manchester Pearl was here,
November 13th 1999

EVOLUTION OF TIME

Me and you, a smile,
From there a kiss,
Then a touch, marriage
And our two gorgeous
Children, a fight, then
The cops, I'm packing
My things, in comes
My replacement, a
Harlem cat, nothing
To envy, a decision
Made by two, a crime
Committed by one, a shotgun,
One bullet, one life sentence,
One man's view on a story
Of two, this is what happens
When time catches up to
Love, my passion
For Gloria will soon fade, if
Life in prison continues

"Everyone is necessarily the hero of his own life story."

– John Barth

REALITY SHOW

Death is a release from a life
Sentence, written in
Fragments, commas and
Question marks, signed
Sealed, and delivered
To inmates, a new life,
Called Jail, featuring the
Devil and his goons, as we lay,
Head pressed sideways to the
Earth's gravel, prayer comes
Over me, when nothing left
To do is available, a mission
Fought, a duty complete, a life
Taken, time served

FORTY ACRES

Erasing the memory of
All bad times to come,
Tragic, yet loveable
Times become harder than ever,
Sudden death brings
A pain more visible now
Than ever, a child's face says
It all, as man tries hard to
Forget the last time he
Or she made love, because the
Penetration from the lover
In question, brings too much
Hurt, so sad, so true we humans
Tend to forget about the
Small things, loved without
Meaning or thought,
love survives all the tragic
Times left behind, so secure in
faith, age seems to be nothing
More than a number, issues
Of you and I, seeking closure
To a life so uncertain, I'm here
For life, you have no choice,
But to trust me

DON'T BE MAD

Through hard times,
Endured happiness occurred
Only but once, from the start,
Love making wasn't worth
Speaking loudly about, a reference
To you not wanting to
Kiss me below is obvious, yet
Childish, in my own time,
I spent more time with
My mistress, who I hold close,
She being all the things you
Were afraid to be, she said the things
you never would,
I love you and I miss you,
For a decade or so, we made love
Three times a week, at best, she
Means more, however with you
Is where I consider home,
Don't be mad, I'm only human

PRACTICALITY

Life inside, the slow
Dryness of death, the reoccurring
Pain in the chest, a battle,
Forever tattooed as life,
Another reason for the
Disposition of Utopia Wright,
Through prayer and faith is
Where I find release, through scripture,
I seek truth, unless referring
To an Arabic text, subtitled
For the Islamic followers parading
This block of the facility, God
Blesses all if you ask me, through
Divine teaching we all can get
To where it is we feel safest,
Through spiritual guidance, maybe
I'll be able to see my kids grow
Into adults, through unfortunate
Timing and misrepresentation,
I will remain here for life praying,
For you and yours

PROVIDED

Through voices of
Children playing silently,
I'm finalizing the understanding
Of the rest of my life, through
Tears shed for the
Many men and woman walking
God's earth, with heads held
High on faith alone, through
The fire and stone breeds
Mischief, violence and
Lustful thinking, through
Chapters of reading the word,
I pause, through and through,
I'm without guidance, if not
With you, through you I see
Through the lies, through you
I see what they see, the make up
Of original man, a special gift
Placed permanently in my hand,
Only to fade to a close, through
Violence I chose this life, through
Sentencing I received life, yet
Still through you, I feel alive
And through you I'm finally
At peace with our God

OUT OF SIGHT

The words of the dead
Echoes loudly through the
Night's whisper, racing to
My brain in a flash, sudden pauses,
Only to replay the horror,
A message I take it, a sign
Of some sort, a reason for
The life sentences, explained
Through voices heard in
The morning's glory, lonely
At times, so unaware of
Life on the outside, I cry,
Through tears, I see things
As clear as a lifer can, no
Turning back or moving on,
I am permanently resting in
The belly of the beast,
I forever am, Utopia

BLACK WORDS

Why not these words here,
They fit fine, expresses exactly what
I intended to say in that court room,
A couple of years prior, terrified by
The court proceeding, asking the same
Questions over and over, these same
Words of "fuck you I'm innocent"
Repeats solo, forever, to a man wanting
Freedom now more than ever, tonight's
Release will only be in my palms,
Together I'm lost, always in the dark
About information overheard, he said,
She said shit, a total of three years
In and I'm losing my mind and all the
Words I'd like to say are no longer
Avail, the same sentences I once
Memorized, have now been pushed
Back further, my pen doesn't want
To work, it refuses, it's black
And it's always in the dark

EVACUATION

The projects paint
A picture seen by
Those familiar, drugs
And guns, nothing new to those
Wanting change, waiting in vain,
The choices of adolescents, the
Decision of judges, grudges and
Gang wars, so raw, those fortunate,
Never once saw the core
Of being poor, unless willing
To relocate and play these games,
The streets consider life, can't
Be me, the street's only villain
Placed in prison for murder,
Not me, the first of the few
Who never knew his father,
The last of the realest men
Alive, through hard tears and
Prayers, most criminals were still
Sent here, only to be confronted by
The others who see ass, oral pleasure
And gangs, the system arranged by the state
Of New York stores the world most wanted
Fathers of inner city children,
A crime in itself, time is the only life line
Left for the strong

KISSING

The last time
We kissed, I saw envy in the
Eyes of my partner,
A sparkle of hate frowned
On her face, hot and steamy,
I still entered her, soft
And wet, she let me feel
Her insides without a
Condom, that bothered
Me most, why wouldn't
She step up and say
Something, lust or not,
Too many died from that
Virus, but I did it
Anyway, kissed her low
And all, so sweet to taste,
I went down again and again,
A true gift, blessed in
Oral, she is my favorite
Fantasy, it is she who
I think of when I touch
Myself, self love to
Those in the business,
I am Utopia, average
At lovemaking, yet gifted
At kissing

QUICKIE

Making love slowly
Under the darkness
Provided by the night,
One drink too many,
She placed her hand
On my thigh, arising the
Beast between my legs,
She begged for it, Her
Eyes said it all as she
Undressed me to a nude,
Patiently staring at the
Body of what she considered
A God, a simple night turned into
A great one, as we touched she
Looked directly into my eyes,
Wanting me, she grabbed at it,
Slowly inserting what most
Would consider a great package,
I grabbed the softness provided
By her ass, at last, a passionate
Feeling ending quicker than
We both expected, she said she couldn't
Hold it much longer, so she let go,
Releasing a moisture so slippery it leaked
Down her Leg, a kiss to the forehead
Explained it all

SOFT SHEETS

Dried up, so weak
From the effort,
A steady flow of
Depression invading
My thoughts, lost is
The life of my
Mother's favorite,
She always addressed
Me as the talented one,
Yet through passing,
I've been losing a battle
Unscripted, wicked how
Time challenges the mind,
This story of mine
Should be heard for
It's truth and reality,
That being my disposition
Towards society, a riot
Of laughter overwhelms me,
I'm forced back into my cell,
Lockdown is living hell,
But somebody has to do it

"Things turn out best for the people who make the best of the way things turn out."

— John R. Wooden

UNITED

The times
Spent behind the
Theory of passion
Filled dreams, seemly
Seems to be the only
Solution to a life
Misled by my mother,
Who lied about the
Whereabouts of my
Father, who I've
Been longing to meet
Face to face since
The first day I
Realized he wasn't around,
At best I must move forward
Without holding grudges
Towards those not
Involved in my
Life's disposition

LIFE

Good times
Smothered my mind,
With false hope of
Seeing my mother's
Angelic features again,
Cooking breakfast
Full of pork and
Grease, the days of
Love, missed by children
On the verge of becoming
Adults, leaving life up to
Us to fuck up, the warmth,
Far gone from the chest
Of her youngest son,
Spending the rest of
His days in prison,
Never would she
Have missed this day if
Not taken away by the
Hateful hands of man,
Until she stands side by side
With her children, I'm for
Surely willing to kill
For all the smiles
And kisses missed by her
Children, in these hard
Times of life living

SOLUTIONS THAT WORK

Gloria, my love for
Life, sure we fight,
Simple shit pisses
Her off, the shower
Door or clothes
On the floor, the
Same things she
Hates, I glorify more
And more, she's loved
By me and those
Involved in her circle,
Due to time, I can't
Hurt her, can't begin
To calculate the reasons
For the hurt, a feeling
Felt at the pit of the
Soul, where love muscles
Hold together the passion
Now missed, for the kids
We live life to a full, hoping
To pull through, if it wasn't
For you, the reader, I'd be dead
Long time, through her eyes,
I see a future, therefore
Gloria is my only solution
To a life lost in an
Institution of cowards
And confusion, I am
Utopia Wright,

UNPARALELL

The life and times of Salem Hussein with
A tear drop imprinted on-his face, a sudden
Reminder of childhood gangsters, bitches and
Malt Liquor, the reliability of prison is amazing,
The irony of it all is improving, young black
Youth are moving at such a rapid pace, leaning
On the bars to survive, teary eyed Muslims
And Arians live together in the same fear as yourself,
Pardon self for crimes committed, whether convicted
For or unseen, I feel born again to live again,
yet trapped in prison to find out why

COMPLEX

God himself said
I'll be the last man
Standing with his
Hands griped tight
On the Holy Book,
A testament of love
Found in His words,
Proving my theory that
God hears all and judges
Not one more person
Than myself, and it
Was during this realization
That I was hand picked
To lead the many lost in
The world today, with
Words as my only tool,
Cowards and fools alike
Will surround me with
Gifts and blessing,
All wanting to understand
The lessons of man

TIER PREACHER

Hell is here, beside me sits the liars and most
Ruthless personalities known to man, the ignorance found
In the words of men, who like yourself walk earth hopeless
In thought, maybe the time given was harsh, or maybe
The life taken was one of your loved ones, no matter
The case, I'm surrounded by weak, fragile youth, lost in
What they assumed was the best time of their
Lives, hanging on them corners with the locals,
Talking that talk, fuck this, fuck that, the usual
Talk of the minor league thugs waiting to bat with
The big boys, little did they know all the real
Big boys are dead or laying up in a penitentiary,
Somewhere cozy, with years and years ahead of them

CHARITY

Boringly
Wanting life to be sucked
From my presence, hopelessly
Wishing death passes me soon,
A feeling contemplated for
Many years now, has finally
Taken it's toll, a movie it is not,
A life so violent must be stopped,
For the better of mankind, my
Time here should be done with,
If left to me I'd end it now, however
There is the wife and children,
Roaming free and in them,
I find all reason for living,
Such an unnecessary sentence
Of life, without the possibility
Of parole for twenty five years

DAILY REALITY

The charm on this one
Is divine, her talent for
Lovemaking is remarkable,
Stunning in all forms
Of being beautiful, she is
The woman I've always
Craved, the attention from
This one proves the dedication
To my disposition, these words
Flow simple when I mention
Her name in text, Gloria Wright,
A woman's gift to society,
Similar to a life
Sentence, she's that much
In tuned with the system,
Trailing that round ass, are
My two children with facial
Features of the Prince
I once was, now I'm King of my
Own vices and issues,
Fully aware of the end
Solution, I will die in these
Prisons, nothing can be done
To prevent that, therefore,
I live what's left of a valued life,
Through the eyes of my wife
And beautiful children

PALMER'S GROUP HOME

A friend was murdered last night, receiving a
Stab wound to the neck, a very disrespectful way
To go, he will never again play the games we shared, Basketball and
women, the average day, now dawned by the Night's violent era, the
motive for his murder was Senseless, like the rest, he lived but only a
few years Longer than my brother, who got lost in the street's
Troubles, some years prior, the last goodbyes to a man Wandering
life in his own tune, a friendly dude, now Subjected to rest perma-
nently in a place many rarely pay Their respects

EVERYTHING IS NOTHING

The peace sought is found
In freedom, the opportunity
To walk amongst the free
Is what arouses me most,
Sexual frustration is
The least of my problems,
I want to get out of here,
I can't do this for life,
I refuse to, I'll take more
Lives if needed, the rage of
A lifer is this, most time
Spent is loving my wife
And kids from behind a
Grim face, a smile most
Inmates will never see,
The beast they've grown
To know is only a small
 Make up of the
Man my mother raised,
I'm amazed at times, how
Cruel and hard my attitude
Can be, I blame the system for
Creating this monster of
A man

COLLECT CALLS

Loving you with all
My days, never looking
Away, nor falling back into
A state of regret, I killed
A lover of yours, granted, he attacked
Me and I shot him, it has been done
Many times over, if not by
Me, then by the many men
Across the world, a man's
Woman is his pride, once that
Has been tampered with or
Stepped on, he would
Never see clearly, woman
Seem to think in detail, we men
React in an instant, that first
Instant usually sends a lot
Of good men to prison,
That's without question

TOWOTA

Yesterday's blisters
Healed in clutch timing,
A grip, scaled with dead skin,
Provided Enough of that, by the bars, I'm
Missing Leonia Ford,
A vixen diva pearled,
Roped and mild,
Handy in conversation,
Spiteful with words, an
Uncertain way about her
Appearance, it just blends
Perfect with the bars,
A teacher by trade,
Partly due to an
Upstate upbringing,
Living single in the
Mountains where time
Freezes man ice cold,
On some days she
Allows me to touch her
Chest, sending me back
To my quarters with
A lustful taste of
What could never be

REGAL SANTANA

The escape from a big
City issue, a remembrance,
Silenced by the moment's
Aroma, a touch of tender
Love, crossing the bridge
To good times, forever
Found in the last exit, reading
East 572, a place where
Surrender is absurd, the
Most one can do is pray,
Where battle is commonly
An unregulated ambition,
Situated into a death, certain
By the age of Eighteen,
The rest are only
A shoulder away from
An endless future in prison,
Where we the men and woman
Of the system would like
To say "Get up, get out
And get over it"

SHADOW ART

Anyone listening should
Understand I'm innocent
Of the many crimes
Presented before this
Courtroom, these bastards
Spit lies, daily the judicial
System displays it's faults,
Flawless for its punishment
And sentencing, I'm a witness
To the disposition of
Utopia Wright, Manchester
Pearls lives through the words
Of my father who I hold close,
Hoping one day we will
Meet to pardon some
Of the old times missed, his
Image reflecting my face, means
Most to a convict on his last
Leg begging for freedom,
We all know will never be granted,
Slow motion for me as time develops
Into a fizz, a blur of nothing beautiful
Or special, just me and
Manchester Pearl's sprit,
holding down life in this box

HEATEDLY PRESSURED

If I ever get out of
This cell, I'm gonna rip
Somebody's head off,
The violence of ole
Has returned, the blackness
In my eyes means war, blood
From ear to ear, a wound caused
By the hounds that collage
This facility, the mostly men
Faculty of hate and havoc,
Endless shanks are
Present, created by the most
Creative people in the world,
Now relocated to live in a cell,
The substance abuse is present,
Many men can't wind prison life
Without a hit, a frustration most
Keep hidden, yet the signs of
Withdrawals are written
In prose on their faces, stoned
On all occasion, house liquor,
Reefer and Bible paper, one lifer,
A wife and two
Beautiful kids at home, a
Time in the life of Utopia,
A day in the night of a
Prison, I am still here,
Alive, yet heatedly pressured

VIA ATLANTIC AVE

Life or lifeless,
The current affair is this,
Stuck here to match the
Time received, flowing like
A stream of self hatred, I'm picturing
Better days, a foolish mind set,
A violent lifestyle
is not hard to please, changing
To please whites, a racial barrier found
In prison, Hispanics and blacks are inferior
to one another, a custom most
are forced to respect, a promise
From the heart, a lover from Brooklyn,
Now an inmate in prison

DIFFUCULTY

The glory in
The faces of black children,
Living ghetto lives in
Genocide areas of Brooklyn,
The gates surrounded hell,
Considered home, the carving
Of poverty in faces of mothers
Trying to build a system the streets
Can't penetrate, because they know
Most about the hoodlums and
Their children, they know best
About these horny teenage boys
Lusting after their daughters,
Just the things known, just the
Things in need of change, just
Me on Thursday.

LIKE MAGIC

Deployed to a grain
Of salt, so pasteurized
It's burns stem on flesh,
Mashing Organs
On contact, blinded,
The curiosity of man,
At on point I decided
To end all life, a knife
Made from metal debris,
Formally known as a
Murder weapon, so wicked,
I spat at them, they being
The guards of this facility,
Everyday it's some new shit,
Am I wrong in my doing? So
Supportive of love I seem
To be the only one knowing,
A secret so good it's hard
To keep close, at lost, I'd
Like to inform the worst
Of love and good times ahead,
But they look at me and laugh,
Knowing their time here
Will be their last, so I
Fall back and remind self
Of my own life sentence,
Suddenly I begin to cry

FUN FOR ALL

Through the nights glow
I'm confused upon which way to sleep,
On my stomach or back, simple shit
Like that, penetrates my every thought,
I'm preparing for a basketball game
Against the police tomorrow,
They can't beat us, we stand tall,
Forced to be locked up, strapped down
For being convicts, detained for
My words, I continue my struggle,
The disposition of a man, Utopia
Wright is just one of the many
Doing life sentences in New York State,
across the country it gets worse,
I can only agree, imagine me
Doing life in a Southern or mid western state,
that's a whole new slang, a new
Way of life, however it's still prison,
I'd still be in custody for the rest
Of my life and my victim will forever
Rest the stiffness, provided by yours truly,
my first kill, the diary of a mad man,
 I am Utopia Wright

BROOKLYN ESTATES

The voice of the people,
I am the man I used to see, the
Truth in the flesh, he being honest
As the rest, so sincere with thought,
A lover in more ways than ever,
So sweet and conscious of others, the
Personality of a saint, not really, so
Smooth with my life, what's left of it,
I'm forwarding my words to a friend,
He then will try his best to spread it
To the world, the disposition of
A man doing life, a sentence
Within a sentence, words of my time
Spent behind these closed walls,
Letting go of meaning, subjected to fight,
To struggle more, yet Brooklyn
Prepared me most for this, if not for that
Borough and those projects,
I'd probably would have fell victim
Like the rest, Therefore through my life,
I'll always respect where
I'm from, the same place you
Fear is where I'd rather be

FREE GLORY

The great things is I love
You with all heart, the reason
I'm the man today, you bring the
Light to such a dark life, so much
Love received, I free you from all
Anger and stress, I'm a man, a
Husband to you, your problems
Become all mine, the scared, the
Frail, the weak, all of the above, will
Never stand in between this
Project love, ghetto as they come,
Smart as the next, intelligence works,
Jabbing me with signs of frustration,
I read all signs, I'm upset that you care,
I hate that I'm loved, hate that
Someone in the free world cares most
About my life, it's so sad, so childish
At times, I am Utopia Wright, the
Same as I was in the free world,
Prison got me early, I didn't get to do all
The great things assumed with my time,
I ended up living proof, so the rest
Can do what they're suppose to do,
And that's a friendly reminder, from a
Lifer, to the free

BREATHING LESSONS

God said these days would
Show signs of relief, forward
We will march, hand in hand,
So demanding of love, we will finally
Understand why we've waited
So long, His voice, that being God,
Was secretive, first I fell to
The floor, unworthy of His speech,
I began to pray, He stood me on my
Two feet and smiled, His features
Similar to my own, so beautiful
I began to cry, moving forward
In a whisper, gravitating me to His
Words, His mellowness and overall sprit moved me,
Unaware of my conscience state I fell to His feet,
Like a child taking his first steps, He extended His hands
Embracing me with His love, suddenly I understood,
Suddenly I was enlightened, suddenly I was alive

CRANIUM

Above ground the violent
Smell of violet flavored
Rain, swallows the night
For the purpose
Of death, an honor
Towards the devil's
Way of living, a sacrifice
Christ wished on no one,
Standing alone in a world
Lovely, yet blue, skies fall,
Nails break at the sight
Of one's fate being tampered
With or should I say handed
To them on a peaceful plate
Of perception, a deception most
Will never overcome, until death
Passes and time erases, my lungs
Will cry blood for the falling, my
Eyes will bleed beer for rest,
At best these words will peak,
Stray and hit home to some,
I am an animal with flesh, a criminal
With time faced, what about you?

LOVE ROLLERCOASTER

Too much of anything
Is great, sex and love
Differs by touch, an understanding
By woman and man, I can't get enough,
Inside her insides, I slide
In and out, a stir motion in that
Ocean of wetness, an erection thick
Like thighs, her eyes says it all,
My darling Gloria, beautiful at pleasing
Me, teasing me, touching me, kissing me,
more and more, she remembers
My spot, screaming ones name because
It feels right, demanding in oral, I'm
On my back receiving the best of Gloria
Wright, locked in, trapped, yet never
Too occupied not to fantasize about
My lovely wife Gloria

THE FIGHT

A forgiveness she wished she could take back,
as the years passed the more children she had,
the more her husband drank, the more she was raped,
undying love was the only reason she cared to stay,
yet the fear of life without her husband frightened
her more than God or Satan, the last stop to a life
lived on her knees, then one day she said
no and he put his hands on her until she no
longer was breathing, the beginning of the end,
now the dangerous streets of Harlem is now
being taken over by the dangerous smiles of the others,
you can't trust it, we are still at war with the people
who look just like us, the truth behind the song
is lacking trust, the protection behind them badges
are not for us, the pointless murders of my brothers
is senseless, yet who am I to preach, I've killed
before and I'll kill again, I smothered the face
of many, but I've grown since, the respect I killed for
doesn't move me anymore, now I pray while teaching
and adding something beautiful back to
my community, the founder of a revolution,
soon to be televised, yet not for the eyes of the
people, but for those who claim we're not equal,
to you bastards I say this, change will come and
change will follow, change will lead us and
change will guide us, if looking for change in the
eyes of a new lover, good luck trying to change a
motherfucker, pardon the harshness, but let's be honest,
most new lovers are already traveling with baggage and
you trying to tell them different will sound foreign,

so keep to yourself and play the game to win,
easy on the bottle and marijuana smoking,
you just might need your liver and lungs for the long run,
I thought time would teach us something in return,
instead it laughed in our faces, all different races will be
faced with the same judgment, this fight will be won
by someone, just not us, yet why am I dying to give,
dying to try, the others see me as a threat, they too
see no hope in fighting, how could I stop,
I'm trying to give my all,
I'm here with God's words tattooed on my chest,
in these days that's all I have left, the streets
will always remain, the real violence begins with us,
why am I dying to live here when death only calls,
I have no answers, I'm more shocked than
anything else, but on the other side of the
struggle, you'll find peace measured by love,
the voices and faces of the young, they too want
better lives in this country, hoping to out live
their parents, the saga will continue, remember me,
remember these words, I prayed and let go,
allowed God to take control, and on that day
I wrote these sentences, hoping it would
make sense to somebody, hoping it would penetrate
the children, hoping to spread God's work, His teachings
and His grace, yet if that doesn't work, I'll hit the streets,
personally I'll teach all those willing to listen,
still I'll be the teacher God expected, the duties of
Satan couldn't make a difference, but it does, the clock
must stop on this man, his preaching is killing the people,
his work is the reason we're still fighting, but I bet you
already knew that, its as clear as the homelessness,
but the dogs on my corner need feeding, so they strapped
up and eat, just hope you're not in their path of destruction,

they only speak the language of the struggle,
while some sit back asking why are people still struggling,
I'll answer that with a stoned face, reasons that be is this,
we are the ones living without from birth, so let's start there,
born into this situation, my mother, father and their
parents before them, the cycle continued, yet the
fight for their lives is to get out before they
take you out, they being us, they being the others,
pick your poison, either way for the rest of
your life you'll have to fight, if not today, maybe
tomorrow, your days may be filled with fighting,
the results are left to you, the people only understand
certain things, Jesus, gold, fancy clothes, cars and rims,
not uncommon, not a joke, these are the cards we were dealt,
now let's overcome this madness, let's show ourselves
that we can make it without all the stereotypes, I am sure
if we come together it we'll get stronger, but if we have to do
it alone, then it starts with us, individually we must do
what we are suppose to do, I thought I would be the only
one, yet I was surprised, the more men and women
I come across who all want change, they all are tired of the fight, many
enemies see us conversing, but they don't have
the balls to interrupt, I dare a coward, I dare a savage, I dare
the others to try, they die looking pitiful, I see them age horribly, the wrinkles
of living such a one sided life, we the people want answers, what were the
reasons for the slave trade?,
what kind of human species would take another and
make them work?, to take, to rape, to steal, to lie,
just the attributes of a savage, I'll leave it at that,
I hate to be that kind of person, I hold no personal
grudge towards no man, I just want answers,
I was told I should just get over it, let's not get crazy,
how does one respond to such ignorance,
my cousin Charlie was a victim of a police shooting,

they shot him twelve times in his back, killed by
three officers of the default color, I personally feel it was
because my cousin was black, but who the fuck am I,
the officers were back on duty in less than a month,
my cousin's funeral was cheap and unfair, just like his death,
yet if I were to find love I'd be more sensitive, if a woman
would tell me her secrets, I'd be more understanding,
if she would allow me to touch her, to tell her how
beautiful she is, the smile and scent of a woman,
the only mission incomplete, the only reason I remain
single is because I haven't found a woman willing
to find with me, a stand up gal, someone to bring home
to momma, I hate to say it, but I doubt I'll find her,
maybe it's the circle of people I'm surrounded by,
maybe if I attended night clubs or church
gatherings, I'd find her, maybe she's waiting in
the wind and I can't see her, her eyes not visible,
her style unseen, her thoughts unrecognized,
Her design unreachable, her timing just perfect
because falling in love at this moment would only
distract our cause, I must be strong for a nation of
men and women in need of guidance, a modern day
leader who doesn't lie, who doesn't play political
games with the people, I seek to honor and uplift all, while staying true to
the foundation that got us here, God's way, His best kept secret just might
be me, and people like me are in demand, providers, instructors, teachers and
children, we must remove the chains before we move the chains, and we
must want change before we can change, this life is the longest trip, the
longest journey unknown to man, extra time served for those in prison, the
mind must overcome the inner pressures from the
government, it's a problem only if you let it be, I personally
don't give a flying fuck, but that's just me, I can recall
ten years ago, they said I fought only for my family while
leaving behind the children of the others, a war against

mankind and I betrayed my country, these were the words
read at my hearing, the military has finally had enough of me,
as if life as a Untied States soldier is a life for a black man,
I fired back, explaining to them that family comes first,
how the others had to fend for themselves,
I once extended my hand, but they refused, momma raised a man,
no fool, so with that said, I left and grabbed my brother's children, I made
sure they had proper care and security, if left up to you, they'd be dead in a
river of water and blood, the silence in the room proved I made my point, the
sentence handed down was an instant reminder I was in America, what do
you know about shooting to live, walking in dirt to hide from the enemy,
the risk involved, the horrific sight of death, body parts and skulls, the
blood of men and women willing to kill to protect your life, the reason why I
can not hate, the reason why I understand the difference between us and
them, the questions is when will it stop, when will it change?
I fought for twenty two years and still
I'm here, the beauty of God's protection, I spent some odd years
following the rules of the land, suffering from the endurance of man, tell me
I'm not wise, make me a believer I beg, please tell
me I'm lying, tell me my faith is fake, tell me I'm lost
behind this pen and I just might agree, yet there's nothing about
this fight that leaves me discouraged, nothing about me fades
when it rains, I'm as clear as water, as visible as poverty, let's not for one
second forget how we got here, those who spared
their freedom and civil rights for you and I, I'm aware of it all,
the beginning, the middle passage and what's left of us today,
yet I know life will continue whether you listen or not,
I know these words won't change them all, but I have
feeling if you made it this far you must want change,
you must feel the way I do on days like this, a man like me only
comes through once in a lifetime, similar to the great men
before me, I feel loved, I feel blessed, my heart is full,
my life is now, today, this very second, tomorrow's sorrow
has yet to come, so for now I'm just doing what I hope to

do tomorrow, be myself during times of depression and
terrorist attacks, God's encore, I am the fight, the struggle,
the reason, the muscle, I enjoy living, the thrill of it,
the unknowing, captured by today's headlines, another young
black male murdered by another young black male, the result of
women, drugs and lack of money, the outcome will always be tragic,
the closer I get to heaven the easier the fight, I try telling myself its none of
my business, it's not a problem of mine
nor my immediate family, yet I can't sit back and watch
Satan ruin the lives of young children, which reminds me
of the tales of Gerry McLean, first born out of fifteen,
a father's pride and joy, through sports and family they raised
this child to be a great man, scholarships led to degrees,
then one night a man found his way into his child's bedroom,
the man then kidnapped, raped her, killed her and left her
body on the side of the road, another typical morning
for the McLean family of four, an early morning workout for
Dad before dawn, breakfast and coffee, as mother
called out to their child she became annoyed by
her daughter's lack of response, so she stomped to
her room to find it empty with no signs of her child,
father is frustrated thinking their daughter is playing a
very bad game of hide and seek, so they storm the house
looking for her, preparing to discipline her for the early
morning charades, an hour later the parent's frustration
becomes worry, once they realized the situation, they
called the local police, they were more than willing to help,
searching high and low for baby Keisha, a parents worse nightmare,
a young child's body found on the side of the road,
a father's last cry, looking at his daughter's naked body in a
puddle of dried up mud waters, a mother's only child killed by
the hands of a child raping savage, the headlines of tomorrow's
morning paper commute, a sad ending to a young life full of promise,
through the days travels, I step to you, looking in both

directions, I asked you what was needed, you replied the corner
needs a changing. I cried, I demanded you give me the
tools needed, you stood directly in front of my face
and laughed, in my lifetime I've never been so
disrespected, not by a black man like myself, a bigger version
of me, yet I know you personally. We sat and ate at the
same dinner table, I am you, never forget the days when mother
carried us both, dragging us side by side down the street,
let's not forget brother, let's remember the small things that
defines us, mother's favorite and all, I'll still smack the
shit out of you, I run this house these days, until you begin
acting like an adult, I will stay on your ass, once you get your shit together,
maybe then the respect level will rise baby bro,
the fight never stops, the tears never dry, the aftermath is
always the same, heartbreak and mourning, I'm full of memories
of those loved and lost, the mothers, fathers and children of
mother and fathers, the gun battles and AIDS victims,
the drug addicted and common day whores, the police who pursue,
the prosecuted and the prisons that house them, an ongoing fight
to the death for those who suffer, whether it be stupidity or
hunger, the reasoning behind the fight is all too common,
but that's not a problem to a problem solver, revolving around
revolvers, stashed in closets, the hardest of the hard has
fallen to the fight, they lose the battle before the knew the struggle, they lost
their lives before they even knew they
were living, so sudden, so un-Christian like, so horrible, so sickening, to pick
on women and children in order to
please ones animalistic cravings, the monstrous
men and women who rape children, the families who
are forced to deal with it, this fight will not be televised,
only those involved will know what's going on,
all updates will be conveyed through family,
one ear to the curb and the other on the police,
we live by a code enforced by each other, from your

sister to my brother, you and I both share the same story,
the same hunger, the same dedication to better ourselves,
can't quite do it alone, naked and without direction, who will guide you to
the truth, who will provide that protection, I've never put too much faith in
celebrities or athletics, I'm in search of a bigger solution to a poverty, drugs
and the other woman, the problems that solve themselves are minimal,
a retaliation towards the powers that be, through God's mercy
we will all be free, just a moment temporarily, but long
enough to breathe, the inner peace we search, the inner space
where we cuddle to keep warm, our home, heaven's gates, God's
decision to spare our lives, all sins and hard times will vanish,
an experience measured by faith, a fate I've come to live with,
a reality of some sort, the game of life is a lonely sport, yet
without a thought I play to find love, I pray to find God because
it's hard, but never have I cheated to win, then again I was
born in February on a dark day for the people, the same day
a man received his freedom, but was killed the same evening,
a man who was wrongly accused for a heinous crime,
later overturned, yet the many years they had him caged
penetrated his faith, he no longer walked with God or
had respect for the law, government and himself, he gave up
on life's blessing the day he was sentenced, when they finally
freed him he went to the old community and noticed
instant change, the difference twenty two years can make,
yet on this same day he sat down at the same bar his
father chose over him and his family, he watched closely
as the owner poured him his whiskey, Brother Billy the
Bartender, he will always remember him, his father's best friend,
his father's killer in a sense, seven shots of whiskey later
the anger of this man's childhood begins, drunk and freshly freed
from prison, this man then jumped over the counter, grabbed
Brother Billy the Bartender and began beating his face with his bare knuck-
les, killing the man he felt put him and his family through all this trouble,
because it was Brother Billy who killed that woman that cold night in

December, let's not forget to
remember it was his darling mother who suffered the most,
while he was in prison she was struggling to feed his siblings,
the man of the house wasn't home, through all the hard times
she endured, she still made it church every Sunday, she
prayed for the safety of her children and husband, never did
she give up faith, upon her son's return home, she waited
for her oldest child to come home, another sad day for a mother
in need of comfort, her life is now a wonder, not to jump off course for a
minute, but I designed a program for the children to follow, a set of rules
needed for survival, only parents should present these regulations, a secret
code between parents and their children, if properly executed we actually
can stop a lot of violence in the future, one day I hope to introduce this plan
to the parents of the world, but first I'll have to start with those in my
communities, they need it most, I must continue, the triumph I chase, a
feeling, a sprit on a level similar to, yet not higher than love, a conflict some
find within themselves, a personal fight between man and his inner self, his
inner voice, the challenge of being wrong, the same as the past, the days of
chains and orders, a tall man versus the small, the strong outlasting the
weak, in my sleep I see Jesus standing with his arms exposed, waiting to
hold us all, the longest time ever, forever I'll be me, the mouthpiece for a
generation of women and children willing to chase dreams, eight million
walking hand in hand demanding the deserving respect from each other, our
fight will not end with rappers, athletes or entertainers, our war is a personal
one, one we must dig deep within to really notice, something we must
overcome if we ever want to attend the graduations of our children, I'm tired
of burying small children of our community, their innocence relocated to a small box
placed in the dirt, a family left to mourn, a life sentence
handed down, another life taken, a slow death for the killer, yet death for him
will come, unless DNA reversals keeps
him alive, he'll never be free, life without freedom, a life
sentence indeed, for most of us we will see the signs
in bright lights, those lost will only notice the dark
dim eyes of Satan, his followers and their home, a garden

view of the beach where children play with fire, their parents
standing there in disbelief, finally convinced that hell
on earth is now, the look on the faces of God's children on
their way to worship, they too saw the signs in bright lights,
the best time is morning when the smell of flesh is so
alarming it causes nose bleeds, the father of the house
greets his children with showers of fire, all the gold diggers
of today beware, father has something special for you,
only through grandmother's prayers, will you be able to
run from the fire ahead, lean forward and be prepared for the burn, a simple
feeling, yet a harsh reality, life after death,
not an album title, yet a realization, please believe it,
it can and will happen, yet I must stay focused,
life provides triangle offenses and man to man
defense, my shots must be accurate, all decisions are left up
to me, to score in this game is hard, to hold the title is tough,
the other team will never make it easy, a designed play
for us to lose, if penetrated properly we can beat the system,
yet we can't have any selfish play, togetherness will get us further, I have
faith in you, I know you and I together can
create a dynasty, a movement of some sort, with love and
understanding we can win, we will win if we all come
together and listen, if we take a second to think things through,
the consequences of all actions, the aftermath of all arguments
and disagreements, the small things like keeping our head up,
recognizing the traps, not allowing ourselves to be beat,
it's a win for us only if we apply the pressure and execute
our game plan, as best we know how, a promise from me to you,
a coach, a player and student of the game, I am dedicated to
seeing us win, if you chose to follow the others, then so be it,
make sure they protect you with their lives because I would,
you being my brother, you being my sister, a common gift of
being black in America, an American dream for some,
it is what it is for others, after three years of touring our

communities of the United States I realized the difference
between poverty and being poor, the difference of needing
and wanting, I see it clearly today as I speak before thousands
of people of all races and languages, I now understand
our God's divine plan and that's for us to all live as one,
as impossible as it sounds, I truly believe in the power of change, fuck
images of hand shaking, hugs and kisses, I'm talking
about raising these children to lead our next generation
of mankind, I'm talking about providing the proper
information and tools at a young age, the truth must
be told first, the souls of those who died for the
cause deserve better, they too spent their time here
on earth teaching, preaching the power of freedom and
equality, if it wasn't for them, I'd be against the fight,
I'd rather sell crack and drink my liquor, have children with numerous women
and continue the cycle of being a stereotypical n word, if it wasn't for
Malcolm, Martin and those with the people in mind, I'd most likely be dead
or doing multiple life sentences, smashing some dude in his face for looking
at me different, just the sudden impulse of a monster, a beast, similar to the street,
I am just like them, yet I chose this holy life and chose to
do something different with my time here, yet in the real world
we know what they think of us, the faces they make when
we enter a room, I was told there's something about
a black man when he enters the room, he's noticeable,
he stands out just because he shines, if not for his riches,
then just for being present, we are that blessed, indeed we
add flavor to the world, a man or woman of color, what would the
world be without us, I'm not talking about crime and
all the bullshit in between, I'm talking about life, imagine
a world of Hispanics, Asians and Caucasians only, maybe it
would work, maybe not, as long as we try, as long as we
don't give up or cave in to the vices and distractions
placed before us daily, its going to take pride, its going to take love and
commitment, similar to relationships, we must be

loyal to one another in order for this to work, truth be told,
I'm scared of failure, scared that its all a waste of time,
however I can't sleep unless I try, unless I attempt to make a
difference with my time here, if I don't, who will, words I choose to live by,
side by side, I see us coming together in song and prayer, with my one wish,
I'd ask for peace on earth, with one more wish I'd ask for all classes to
become one, only in a
perfect world, some would say, I agree, yet today I'm greeted
by the likes of Jesse Jackson and Al Sharpton types, they too
want me to spread the words of the fight, hopefully we can provide a visual
for the people who can't see how we live in our
communities, a closer stare at the sun shining on the
faces of our children, the prayers heard through the night,
from door to door you will find at least two to three people
praying to their God for something better than this, some pray
for a new start while others pray for the lives of their children,
they being the ones who will have to find their way
through it all, the gangs, drugs and disease, lack
of money, education and support, makes it ten times harder
to think positive, a reality for those who live here, for them
I pray, for them my fight is there, if they got beef, so do I,
just the lean on me attitude I was raised by, the it
takes a village quote, I've embraced, yet today's focus is
on the future of the culture, some care, others don't,
time will tell, America knows, the rest of the world sees it,
the dry dirt that clings to clothes and skin found
in hampers throughout the inner city, is apart of the fight,
the resistance, the police, the government and their laws
and regulations, the church and their goals, the savages
who rape and kill, the cowards who ran, the men
who stayed, the children who played through it all, the war we adults
understand clearly, the results that changes our lives,
I never thought the word positive could convey so
much pain, while negative provides us with another chance,

the opposite of what we learned as a child, whipped and
beaten for less, scolded and confronted by
parents in public, the humiliation of us children,
yet as adults now we can see what it was all for,
the extension cord abuse, most were subjected to, the pots,
pans and hot irons we ducked from, yet today we must
understand the most important task, which is to do better
than those before us, if not we lose again and I don't know
about you, but I'm living to win, I'm fighting for the same reasons, I'm most
likely the first person who you'll see on the front line, preparing for a
honorable death, picture something different and you'll won't be referring to
me, I stand as a man willing to end his own life for his people, a man deter-
mined to see us do better, just one of those brothers with a little bit of
Martin and Malcolm running through him, I question whether I've invested
my life to a cause underdeveloped, the aftermath of life after the civil rights
movement, if left to me I'd prove it, but it's up to the people to believe it, I've
seen it personally, the war between two worlds separated by race, religion
and money, the result of pig headed, absent minded decisions made by the
others, I can't sit here and cry about it, I'd rather touch those willing to
listen, similar to the late great Utopia Wright, I stood tall as the others spat
in my face, their ignorance and stupidity, I am irreplaceable, according to
some, yet the truth is I'm just like you, as human as the rest, but I still see
you don't know about me, I'm the son of Gerald and Francine Moore,
adopted as an infant, taken in with love, they too saw me as their own,
my siblings alike, yet growing up black in a white household took its toll,
once I was at the age of understanding, things changed,
I began to rebel, to be honest it was the only way,
I was hungry for change, the romance of a killer
with a masters in lovemaking, the anger followed by the struggle,
the proof found in the eyes of my parents, what is the meaning
for all the lies and mistrust, the business of being broke,
the riches of being poor, as days began getting dark, I saw
further into the light, as poverty controlled the city, I flew
to higher ground, the articles in the paper reads as follows,

another man found slain in the backyard of his home, his cock
stuffed In his pocket, his mouth full of semen, I believed in this headline, I
trusted in this system until the day the men, who were guilty of this crime,
were set free, Nassau County's finest never even seen the inside of a prison,
no holding cell, no handcuffs or finger prints, and on that day I realized what
was going on, if it wasn't for being black, I'd be President, but if not I'd be
me, the counselor to a prisoner, his last words spoken in chalk, his teacher
made and example of him, I'll never disrupt class, she was the last person he
killed, shot her to death after school, he hated her, she always picked on him,
he made sure it never happened again, I spoke to him the day before
he took her life, we discussed the after life of life in
prison, if he killed her, he didn't care, he just wanted her dead,
he wanted to see her beg for her life, to look her in
her eyes, as her life was taken, that was his goal, to kill
Mrs. Archer, to make sure she never made another student
feel as small as she made him feel, a focus no man, woman,
parent or law enforcement agent could come between, a fool to
some, yet to me a confused young man in need of revenge, the rest
of his life now belongs to the state of New York, a lose/lose
for him and his family, as long as Mrs. Archer no longer lives,
he feels his fight was worth the time received, I pray for that
child everyday, his cries I hear through the evening lights,
the darkness he lives, I understand, the back pages to his
life story will be noticed, the words he can no longer speak will
be remembered, the rain will erase all the blood lost, all the
drugs consumed, a tall order for some, yet a blessing
for the blessed, I see clearly I'm supposed to be next on
this long list of those in pain, I remember the day I was put here, I was so
young, so innocent, yet I knew from the beginning
the fight was on, but I'm just trying to do me, trying to be the
man in a life full of children, the hustle, the street's passionate way of telling
you that you will die here, the babies who grow into animals, waiting their
turn at the corner, to do better than their brother, uncle and father before
them, the energy to provide more money for their mother, who raised

at least ten of them, the strong will always find a way to
provide for mama, just the finer things we chase
with eyes focused on days beyond the poverty situation,
we the mighty, live in today, the urgency to do better, a reliability placed on
ourselves, never to starve, always have and
never snitch, a code that separated the men from the bitches,
the rats from the stand up, the clones from the real, I suggest you leave and
never come back, a latex can't prevent the diseases
ahead, the days of emptiness, the dryness of defeat, I challenge
any man to live like me, to do right, to walk this way,
so emotional with my reason for fighting, the hustlers and pimps
won't understand until they're facing time, usually it takes a life sentence for
man to really understand and realize the trap,
the streets calling will leave you dead or in jail, yet we've
been saying this ever since we received our freedom,
what the fuck does a man have to do for you to realize the truth,
the honesty in the words written is a pleasure, I do this
for a reason, I chose you, the reader, because it's you I write for, your
mother, her mother and the man who knocked her up, is
why I continue practicing positive energy, because without
you, I'd never be able to create elevation, in your
smile, I see children, through your actions, I see me,
alone and childish, desperately seeking attention
from family and friends alike, I've been there more than once,
made my first mistake at twelve, made the papers with
my first pistol and made the news with my second, Brooklyn born
and raised, yet I stayed home on weekends, just so trouble
wouldn't follow, yet someway somehow, it always did,
the game followed me to sleep, even my dreams were crazed,
shootings, stabbings, drugs and rape, the sex only
made things worse, a child aborted when
I was fourteen, a man's semen traveled, a child's life
unknown, walking closer to the death predicted by my brother,
his life slaughtered by the streets, his mother laughed,

our father cried, his last words of "heroin kills", said it all,
the desire that took over him, his whole life sheltered,
until his first day of College, that's where he learned who he was, a friend
introduced him to cocaine, the beginning of doom,
how difficult to watch the destruction of a family member,
I truly adored, people lined up to view his body, his mother
played the back with a grin on her face, the devil in her showed,
she hated him, him being the love child of our father,
a father who hit us, on repeat, looped for his personal pleasure,
it made me tougher, yet it hurt my mother the same, other than
her hips, she had nothing going for her and my father took
full advantage of it, I heard it through the walls, a sexual beast, three maybe
four times a night, he had to have it and she
had to give it to him, take a deep breath, it will grow on you,
my childhood definitely took some getting used to, once I approached the
civilized age of being an adult, I noticed it wasn't hard, not having, wasn't
the end of the world, all the parties I missed, usually ended up with someone
dying, therefore it was a blessing I couldn't attend, I begin to wonder how
many of us kids, growing up in on that dangerous block, still live at
home with their parents, how many of us actually made something
out of our lives, I'm sure the girls went on to make babies, by men they hate
and I'm sure the boys moved on to prison or death, but the ones who made
it, I thank you for breaking the cycle, for keeping dreams alive by showing
and proving, action speaks volumes, but words travel further, hit harder and
at times, cause wars, the results are evident, for some of us the evidence
of abuse was very visible, for others we hid the signs,
decorated the scars, overdressed to keep the swelling down,
the lies we told to our friends, teachers and counselors,
the fear of our parents was a reality, the fear of the police
is a reality, the fear of being broke with children, the fear of
being gun down on one of these street corners, the fear of being
stabbed to death over a lover, the fear of someone
else's jealousy and rage, the fear of doing life in a cage,
the fear is present, the truth is hidden, the practice of

discipline is under rated, the reason we fight is a promise
that was made before our time, the rest is up to us, we are
here to continue what our fathers and mothers fought for, "we shall over-
come", said best by the best, striving for perfection
with our eyes wide shut, following trends, men and
women who lost their history of self, some made money
and it took control, while others just don't give a fuck
about nobody, but themselves, to them the fight has
been won, the last bell has been rung and the children
are free to follow their dreams, I've seen these type
of fools gathering to appreciate their God given talents,
the money hungry magnets who gave up on their own,
I suppose those men and women are to be looked
up to as role models of some sort, speaking only of
our entertainers and athletes in the United States,
a great opportunity arose and they took it, who wouldn't,
therefore blame is only placed on those who aren't
doing what they're supposed to do, some see a man,
some see a child missing his mother, I see a person,
I am a challenge, a challenged child, now seeking
God to keep me safe, only through Him will I be myself,
mainly because these streets burn flesh on sight,
a war I've been fighting for years, miles from here you will find the truth, I
buried it in the dirt, running from the police,
I felt it would be safe, hidden deep in God's surface,
the land of the free, in my sleep I see demons pointing fingers,
the smell still lingers, the scent of a woman this is not,
the aftermath of a year and a day spent in a hole,
the rebirth of a man in need of God's love, His touch,
His words changed me, I went from hate to love,
from drugs and fast women to prison, from there
He carried me home and placed me back in Brooklyn, where
He feels I belong, yet the temptations of the corner still remains, I still feel
that urge to play, the feeling of that fast life still runs through me, the drama,

the hustle, the corner,
a place that will make or break you, I have to stay
focused, must stay on top of the world if I plan on living here,
can't strive for anything less, the hunger to be the best,
the drive to become a leader, a strong speaker and a
honest teacher, I work hard, I study hard, I love reading, another one of
God's precious, a jewel, a diamond, a king, if not for faith, where would I be,
who would I be, I speak only of
what I do, what I know, what I feel is the truth, the opinion
of a man who cares, a man who honors thy father and
son with love and respect, what's really coming between
that kind of bond, that kind of relationship is built on
understanding that life here on earth will not be the
same as in the afterlife, therefore what we going to do
with our time here, I don't know about you, but
I'll continue raising awareness to all those willing to listen,
the fight

THE AUTHOR

The Disposition of Utopia Wright is the story of Rahson's unknown father. It's a journal from Utopia's point of view. What Rahson has done is taken pieces of what has been and woven it with what could have been, in order to let the world know the story of his unknown father, Utopia Wright.

Rahson Sumter's other publications:

The Unheard Voices of Jamison Pratt
As We Lay: The Ramada Slim Diary
The Sharmy Mcloud Journal
Murder He Wrote: The Fled Williams Story
The Endless Commute of Guy Parsons